# Peace Be with You, Rest in Peace

# Peace Be with You, Rest in Peace

Using Scripture to Address
Spiritual Distress near the End of Life

*Sue Witty*

Foreword by Don E. Saliers

WIPF & STOCK · Eugene, Oregon

PEACE BE WITH YOU, REST IN PEACE
Using Scripture to Address Spiritual Distress near the End of Life

Copyright © 2020 Sue Witty. All rights reserved. Except for brief quotations in critical publications or reviews, no part of this book may be reproduced in any manner without prior written permission from the publisher. Write: Permissions, Wipf and Stock Publishers, 199 W. 8th Ave., Suite 3, Eugene, OR 97401.

Wipf and Stock Publishers
199 W. 8th Ave., Suite 3
Eugene, OR 97401

www.wipfandstock.com

PAPERBACK ISBN: 978-1-7252-7649-9
HARDCOVER ISBN: 978-1-7252-7650-5
EBOOK ISBN: 978-1-7252-7651-2

*Cataloguing-in-Publication data:*

Names: Witty, Sue. | Sailers, Don E., foreword writer.

Title: Peace be with you, rest in peace : using scripture to address spiritual distress near the end of life / Sue Witty, with a foreword by Don E. Sailers

Description: Eugene, OR: Wipf and Stock Publishers, 2020 | Includes bibliographical references.

Identifiers: ISBN 978-1-7252-7649-9 (paperback) | ISBN 978-1-7252-7650-5 (hardcover) | ISBN 978-1-7252-7651-2 (ebook)

Subjects: LCSH: Church work with the terminally ill | Terminally ill—Religious life | Pastoral care | Terminally ill | Spirituality

Classification: BV4338 W58 2020 (paperback) | BV4338 (ebook)

Manufactured in the U.S.A.    11/24/20

*For*
*Don Saliers,*
*with infinite gratitude*

*Your life and your song*
*have been,*
*are,*
*and always will be*
*a lamp unto my feet and a light unto my path.*
*With immense precision and incomparable grace*
*you have taught exceedingly well*
*that*
*"the world is charged with the grandeur of God . . . ."*
*And that has made all the difference.*

*"Listening is loving."*

HECTOR AND THE SEARCH FOR HAPPINESS,
SCENE 18 (2014)

# Contents

| | | |
|---|---|---|
| Foreword by Don E. Saliers | | ix |
| Preface | | xi |
| 1 | A Modest Concern: The Current Model of U.S. Chaplaincy | 1 |
| 2 | An Elaboration of the Dilemma | 7 |
| 3 | Encounters: Patient Relations, Artifact Analysis | 16 |
| 4 | Reflections | 34 |
| 5 | The *Ars Moriendi* and COVID-19 | 44 |
| 6 | Humble Conclusions | 56 |
| Appendix | | 59 |
| Bibliography | | 73 |

# Foreword

How can the emotional and spiritual distress of hospital patients be adequately addressed? What is the role of religious tradition and belief in such care? What are emerging models and practices in chaplaincy that may use the Scriptures in caring for terminal cancer? Sue Witty's book addresses these questions.

The work of hospital chaplaincy is demanding, especially in large urban hospitals. The author, Sue Witty, knows this well and has thought deeply about the complexities of ministry in the context of medical technology and issues of religious diversity. In these pages she gives us a detailed portrait through case studies of her reflection on end-of-life ministry. As both a member of a palliative care team and as ordained clergy, she raises important questions about explicit and implicit uses of Scripture in pastoral care in the face of mortality.

At the heart of her concern are the patients—their fears, anxieties, and the actual way in which various uses of Christian Scriptures may make a difference in their coming to terms with suffering and death. Central to her study is a critical assessment of the "ministry of presence." This form of ministry remains a dominant mode in clinical pastoral education and hospital chaplaincy. In a series of first-person case studies, Witty explores the wide range of specific responses to the art of using Scripture well. These cases reveal a real and often subtle set of patient-chaplain interactions showing

### Foreword

the way in which specific texts evoke and express both comfort and challenge. This moves beyond the "generic spirituality" found typically in more secular hospital practices that seek to avoid religious specificity. We see here how adequate attention to a given patient's state of mind and spiritual temperament can lead to transformational encounters with apt—though often spontaneous—choices of shared Scripture.

While intent on providing comfort and peace for the patient, the outcomes in most cases presented here go well beyond "Hallmark card" images of serenity. Sue Witty knows her Kübler-Ross and more recent literature in pastoral care. There is an honest and even transformational possibility shown in her accounts. I am reminded of the classic spiritual tradition of *ars moriendi* (the art of dying well) in her work. There are, of course, theological and pastoral issues generated by these case studies and her proposed model of practice. While this book does not seek to explore these issues in detail, *Peace Be with You* makes a fine contribution to a crucial dimension of hospital chaplaincy. The re-appropriation of Christian Scripture in the process of ministry to the dying is a welcome development.

> Don E. Saliers
> Theologian-in-Residence
> Candler School of Theology
> Emory University

# Preface

In autumn, 2019, I gathered my DMin doctoral research together along with an accompanying cogent proposal to submit to publishers for consideration. Little did I know that, lurking around the proverbial corner, a pandemic was warming up in the bullpen. I embarked upon efforts to publish this analysis of contemporary US chaplaincy, oblivious to the fact that our entire way of existing in the world would dramatically alter within a matter of months.

By March of 2020, our nation was in the throes of COVID-19. Chaplain ministers (like all ministers) were forced to change the "game plan" of their approach to ministry within their given contexts: hospitals, nursing homes, people's private residences, and so forth. During these early weeks of our country's "lockdown," I naturally pondered whether my prior research had been essentially nullified by the global crisis.

Yet within several weeks, as chaos became a bit of a norm, it was noted in newspapers, magazines, and online publications that "the amount of positive attention health care chaplains have received from the media during this pandemic has been extraordinarily affirming."[1] With every chaplain-centric article I read, and with every conversation involving family members, nursing home staff, or funeral home directors, an awareness dawned that the ideas inherent in my doctoral

---

1. *Chaplaincy Innovation Lab*, May 18, 2020 (https://chaplaincyinnovation.org/chaplaincy-in-the-news), accessed on May 21, 2020.

project about chaplaincy had only become increasingly timely and poignant. The publicity and affirmation of chaplaincy stirred within me a sense that we have become emboldened, now more than ever, to "grow"—that is, to improve—our ministerial practices.

Chaplains had been thrust into circumstances in which the death toll skyrocketed astronomically. And although we may feel well-trained and well-prepared to minister to end-of-life circumstances, this unique socio-historical situation called for an inevitable immediate shift in our priorities and a fresh re-creating of our approaches. The unprecedented amount of ministry to death-and-dying within an extremely condensed timeframe fostered alternate means for what chaplaincy entails.

Thus, significant questions sprang forth in my mind:

- How do we and how can we honor each individual's spiritual and/or religious needs when so many people are dying so fast?
- What is the best way to be attentive to each person's spiritual needs or desires amidst this historic, rampant spread of an obscure infectious disease as that person lay on the precipice of death?
- How should we best engage the "ministry of presence" now?

This last question had actually been the very crux of my research all along. The aspiration to honor individuals' spiritual needs and desires as mortality draws to a close had been the core of my longing from the outset.

It is true that the hope of developing rapport with an individual prior to determining an excerpt of Scripture appropriate to her/his needs became "wishful thinking" amidst the pandemic, since time among the dying had accelerated to warp speed. The time required to build that type of rapport seemed to have become a privilege no longer afforded to any chaplain. And yet, the thought struck me that if we are able to ascertain people's *dying requests* (as it were, quite literally) with only hours or days to bring those supplications forth, then surely the skill set developed in response to urgency, propriety, and necessity could be transferred to times of

## PREFACE

relative peace when the prospects of building rapport and planning out a calmer, more methodical ministerial response could resume.

And thus, with the deeply treasured encouragement of my Candler School of Theology faculty, the results of my research and my passionate convictions follow....

1

# A Modest Concern
## The Current Model of U.S. Chaplaincy

OUR SOCIETY HAS CONFRONTED innumerable unanticipated changes as of late. And with all of the creative approaches to ministry that were subsequently birthed, certain aspects inherent in the general role of the chaplain remain constant. The contemporary image of the hospital/hospice chaplain is remarkably multifaceted, as it has been for several decades now: a minister with an interfaith approach; a member of an interdisciplinary team who provides emotional/spiritual support to patients/families/staff while contributing "sensitivity to multicultural and multifaith dynamics" to all encounters and visits;[1] one who strives to convey a non-judgmental affect while providing strong active listening skills to those in need.

Additionally, chaplains minister to a veritable cornucopia of ailment or crisis situations, generally defaulting to a "ministry of presence" and active/reflective listening in any and nearly all circumstances. Ultimately, they are expected to assist individuals and families face the reality of our own mortality in the midst of incredible medical advancements via a gentle, calming presence. Whenever possible, they—we—strive "to help people die within

---

1. Nussbaum, "Interdisciplinary Teamwork: The Role of the Chaplain," 45.

## Peace Be with You, Rest in Peace

the awareness of being loved; . . . to invite dying with grace and gratitude for the life lived."[2]

For years, I engaged in the ministry of presence without a second thought. This periodically involved bearing witness to people struggling with terminal agitation and existential distress. Perhaps due in part to my involvement with our palliative care specialists, I eventually began to wonder about potential alternative approaches to chaplain ministry that might help assuage the anxiety and distress I was seeing. Something about the ministry of presence model felt ambiguous,[3] even hollow at times. Pondering other approaches soon became quite a distraction. Moreover, when I shared my musings with beloved mentors and seminary professors, their affirmations encouraging exploration of this train of thought came in almost the same breath as them noting that Scripture seems to be dying in this country. It appeared to be no small coincidence that the ambiguity of the chaplain role began nagging at me at precisely the same time highly respected theological scholars lamented the plummeting biblical literacy of our society.

I deduced that what might be beneficial at this time is a study that acknowledges the strengths and positive aspects of the ministry of presence, affirming its validity for the vast majority of chaplain encounters, while asserting that adults coping with a terminal situation (such as an end-stage cancer diagnosis) who express specific spiritual beliefs might benefit tremendously from chaplain visits in which the chaplain assumes a more assertive/direct approach that utilizes the Scripture from that patient's faith tradition. Such methodology could assist individuals in confronting their own mortality, thereby assuaging any spiritual or existential distress they may be experiencing. With this assertion, the study seeks to explore certain basic, significant theological questions: How do we, the professional chaplains, honor each individual's spiritual/religious needs

---

2. Siler, *Letters to Nancy*, 47.

3. See Hutt, "The 'What Is' and 'What If' of Chaplaincy." The Rev. Hutt avers that the figure of the chaplain is—and always has been—ambiguous: "In secular institutions such as hospitals, prisons, and the military, the chaplain's role remains ambiguous since, unlike doctors, guards, or soldiers, the chaplain is an explicit broker between the sacred and the secular."

## A Modest Concern

to the best of our abilities in the days shortly preceding death? What is the most ideal way for a chaplain to be attentive to each person's spiritual needs or desires as s/he lay on the precipice of death? In short, what can we do differently that may in fact be better?

As much as I value the standard chaplain ministry of presence, I have come to believe there are certain times in which it proves insufficient in facilitating a direct confrontation with end-of-life anxieties/fears. And I know I am not alone in such ruminations. Some have publicly questioned, "Can a patient deal with his/her spiritual issues *without* [theological] conversation?" only to conclude that "more research is needed here."[4]

With the realization that others felt as I did, I endeavored to develop this study to explore this area of needed research. The hypothesis is this: Those suffering from end-of-life spiritual anxiety/distress may experience the type of healing that "manifest(s) itself as peacefulness, acceptance, [and] better coping" before they die through the pragmatic incorporation of Scripture into select pastoral care visits.[5] To reiterate, the incorporation of Scripture into *select* chaplain visits should indeed be *pragmatically* determined. Spiritual and existential distress is of immense concern, not only to ministers, but also to medical professionals, family members, lay people, etc., and it therefore begs for our help. Yet it must be noted that the fine line continues to exist between pragmatic incorporation of Scripture into visits and actual proselytizing amid impending death. This study in no way advocates for proselytization. The focus aims specifically at *certain* circumstances, judiciously discerned, in which spiritual distress may be assuaged—and peace instilled—by Scriptural affirmations and words of comfort. The goal always involves keeping in synchronicity with the virtues and aspirations of the Clinical Pastoral Education (CPE) model while striving to meet the spiritual needs of those who may only have days or weeks left to live.

In 1969, Elisabeth Kübler-Ross noted, while focusing on patients at the end of their lives, that "we may achieve peace—our

---

4. O'Connor, "Making the Most and Making Sense," 36.
5. Puchalski, *A Time for Listening and Caring*, x.

own inner peace . . .—by facing and accepting the reality of our own death."[6] Slightly over fifty years ago she perceived that people in the US confronting terminal illness experience a significantly lonelier, more "mechanical, and dehumanized" circumstance due to medical advancements and "life-saving" interventions.[7] This pervasive quandary—which seems to have grown ever more severe over time—provides the impetus for this study. A theological concern functioning in tandem with this problem is that hospital chaplains—as ordained, endorsed, and oftentimes board certified ministers—must be able to "recognize when there is great disparity between present practices and God's Word," and must "work diligently and with deliberation to bridge that gap."[8]

Yet it seems that, in many ways, chaplaincy has become a fairly watered-down practice—to the extent that patients and their families may have no awareness or understanding that the person fulfilling the chaplain role is indeed a minister. Many chaplains are encouraged throughout the educational process (of internships and residencies) to introduce ourselves to patients and family members as one who "provides emotional and spiritual support." The intent of this vague self-identifier is honorable, as it strives to afford respect and dignity to all who may benefit from such support, regardless of backgrounds, faith traditions (or lack thereof), and belief systems. But consequently, chaplains are at times mistaken for social workers, case managers, or even doctors due to the ambiguity of the self-introductions and practices when visiting with patients and families. Instances can—and do—arise in which it would behoove chaplains to utilize semantics of greater specificity in our self-descriptions in order to bridge the gap between our practices (in our ministry of presence) and God's Word.

The efforts of this study are concentrated within one urban hospital context in Philadelphia.[9] However, I propose that this in-

6. Kübler-Ross, *On Death and Dying*, 31.
7. Kübler-Ross, *On Death and Dying*, 21.
8. Strawn, "The Designated Reader Revised," Sermon.
9. At the time of this research project, my context for over a decade had been a Level 1 Trauma Unit hospital with a maximum inpatient capacity of nearly a thousand beds, in a region that historically has strong Catholic,

## A MODEST CONCERN

formation could in theory be applicable to other contexts nationwide, given that many chaplains throughout the country are trained under the pedagogical approach endorsed by the Association for Clinical Pastoral Education, Inc. The method I have explored honors and respects the "ministry of presence" model while probing deliberate ministerial approaches, strategies, and conversations with individuals being cared for by a palliative care team on an inpatient basis who have *self-identified* as Christian (because I am a Christian, and this is my area of knowledge). My purpose in exploring alternate ministerial techniques is to ascertain whether the incorporation of scriptural reassurances in chaplain visits might *positively* impact an individual's emotional/spiritual state of being and welfare prior to her/his death. The parameters of this study involve a focus on the patients themselves—not their families or support systems—who have been informed by the medical team that their situation is terminal and that a palliative treatment plan theretofore would be more judicious than "aggressive medical measures." The execution and assessment of this project incorporated *observable verbal and nonverbal* feedback into the process of determining which Scripture passages (and under which circumstances) potentially possessed the ability to resolve spiritual distress for each given individual.

To be sure, a chaplain in any context must be cognizant of the reality that every hospital and nursing care facility is different from the next, with unique aspects ranging from the socioeconomic and sociocultural profiles of the general patient population to patient satisfaction scores to how research-oriented the medical staff and/or the institution might be. Thus, each chaplain benefits from a multitude of practices—*not* just one approach. Ministers must constantly discern their methodology amidst their own evolving degree of pastoral authority, and ought also "check it out" with their peers.[10] Even so, in my estimation, it is the over-reliance on

---

Protestant, and Jewish roots with ever-increasing Muslim, Hindu, and Buddhist communities.

10. I hold in high regard the action-reflection-action process. As such, I believe we are beholden to sharing our processes with our ministerial peers in order to ascertain their feedback and insights.

the "ministry of presence" that can at times (perhaps inadvertently) cause one to neglect important ministerial opportunities to address a spiritually oriented patient's expressed concerns. And when that occurs, the existential anxieties may persist, causing emotional suffering and spiritual distress that could have been avoided or resolved had other ministerial approaches been employed.

It is my deep conviction that if we *permit* individuals to die in a state of spiritual or existential distress, then we as ministers are guilty of engaging in a grave disservice. Our commitment to our ordained status requires—in fact, demands—much more from us. It is paramount that we facilitate a sense of peace, resolution, and reconciliation in end-of-life circumstances to the greatest extent possible, and that we come to understand that responsibility as part of our ordination covenant.

In the pages that follow, I will first clarify the perceived potential problems of an *over*-emphasis on the ministry of presence in chaplaincy practices.[11] Then I will present an alternative model in select visits that incorporates intentional interventions on the part of the chaplain by reading Scripture passages with patients. This will be followed by a section that covers the data gathered, with a subsequent analysis of that data. The fifth section will reflect upon chaplaincy practices during the dawning of the COVID-19 pandemic, drawing comparisons to the era of the bubonic plague's impact on ministry primarily as an impetus for the creation and mass-distribution of the *Ars Moriendi*. And finally, I will then develop some conclusions for further consideration and propose suggestions for future work/research.

---

11. This project was originally completed in the spring of 2018, before COVID-19 pandemic concerns began plaguing this country. With the spread of the coronavirus throughout the U.S. in the spring of 2020, the role of the chaplain shifted dramatically. I have modified the next chapter in order to include pandemic considerations.

2

# An Elaboration of the Dilemma

MANY PEOPLE HAVE PRECONCEIVED notions about what a chaplain is. I imagine that is the reason I feel much more comfortable nestled in the ambiguity of an introduction in which I emphasize that I am "here to offer emotional and spiritual support." The vagueness helps me skirt the uncomfortable, awkward, or even defiant reactions I might otherwise get. I have witnessed firsthand the shift in people's facial expressions when I've used the word "chaplain." The sudden fear enveloping them is palpable. "Why is the chaplain here?!" they defensively demand. My best efforts at backpedaling and attempting to "talk them off the ledge" of anxiety that the term "chaplain" invokes only fall short. I vividly recall one patient immediately responding to my self-introduction with, "Get out of here! I'm not dying!" Even humor-type or a concierge-type of approach ("I just wanted to see how you're doing today," "Is there anything I can do that would be helpful?") aimed at diffusing tension cannot undo a lifetime of perception.

Needless to say, the image people tend to maintain about the role of the chaplain invokes theological *fear and trembling*. Synonyms such as the "Grim Reaper," the "Angel of Death," "Dark Angel," and "Divine Messenger" periodically drift into my ears from friends and healthcare professionals. As diligently as some of us persist in striving to break the stereotype of what it means to be a chaplain, these notions endure. That is why I have chosen to explore the contemporary model of hospital chaplaincy, which I believe is in many ways pertinent to the hospice chaplaincy realm, as well.[1]

## CONTEMPORARY STATUS QUO CHAPLAIN . . .

To provide a brief background, the model of chaplaincy that has developed over the past several decades emphasizes a "ministry of presence" involving a "generic spirituality . . . [that] respects religious and spiritual diversity"[2] and discourages chaplains from scriptural discourse due to its risk of sounding "preachy" or even judgmental. Chaplains are generally trained, instructed, and expected to be skilled active/reflective listeners, and are *strongly* advised to "keep God language" out of the equation. Dating back to 1925, the history of the formation of Clinical Pastoral Education informs us that the original goal of hospital chaplaincy was to "break down the dividing wall between religion and medicine."[3] Anton Boisen's vision was quite research-oriented (not pastoral

---

1. In the past fifteen years, I have served as both a hospital and hospice chaplain. Though each type of chaplaincy has its unique qualities, the reflections and suggestions put forth in this project could be suitable for either type of ministry.

2. Verhey, *The Christian Art of Dying*, 65. Verhey identifies the "generic spirituality" as an ambitious means of striving to respect religious and spiritual diversity in various contexts. The entire quote chastises this model, raising questions about its appropriateness in twenty-first-century chaplaincy: "this generic spirituality refuses to name the Mystery because it wanted to respect religious and spiritual diversity, but generic spirituality can have an ironic result; it is not finally hospitable to difference. When 'spirituality' is reduced to some lowest common denominator, to something like 'the Ultimate Mystery,' then the ways in which it is named can be trivialized." This sentiment pinpoints the struggles I have experienced in my own chaplain ministry. This "lowest common denominator" ultimately ignores/disregard the specific needs of our patients—particularly those coherent enough to realize their own death is near. The only specific religious need we seem to honor with any frequency is the need for a Catholic priest for Anointing/Sacrament of the Sick.

3. Leas, "A Brief History," ACPE website.

## An Elaboration of the Dilemma

per se),[4] incorporating Rogerian-based person-centered therapy principles into patient visits.[5] And indeed, it seems true to this day that for the vast majority of chaplain visits, a "ministry of presence" is the best approach for meeting patients where they are, for earning their trust, for helping to lessen their anxieties about their ailments, and for avoiding the imposition or judgment that a religious tone can set.

However, for a chaplain to *remain* in "ministry of presence" mode amidst those certain encounters with individuals who are cognizant of their own imminent death could be perceived as a ministerial *disservice* to the dying person. When people are counting their remaining days or weeks, and are consequently experiencing considerable anxiety (either terminal anxiety or existential/spiritual distress), a *strong, confident* ministerial presence willing to identify and name Scripture passages that resonate with the patient's internal core is of infinitely greater value to that individual than the quieter, more reticent role of the active/reflective listener. Such silence and passivity fail to deliver adequate ministry to those preparing to die— particularly in the event when the chaplain is the only minister they have (for example, if s/he "fell away" from church years prior).

Part of an ordained minister's role is to help individuals address and resolve theological, existential, and/or spiritual concerns they harbor. The *Ars Moriendi*, as well as the recent resurgence of interest in it, point explicitly and lucidly to this belief.[6] Clergy are

---

4. Based on the information in the ACPE: "A Brief History" document, Boisen was at odds with his successor at Worcester State Hospital, Carroll Wise, for "changing the program from a research to a pastoral emphasis."

5. Bartley, "The Pastoral Applicability of Person-Centred Therapy," 1–3. Bartley notes that this model, which has been the bedrock of CPE for the past 50+ years, emphasizes the counseling qualities of congruence, unconditional (non-judgmental) positive regard, and empathic understanding, which can help patients become more relaxed, less anxious, and more aware of the root cause(s) of their anxiety.

6 The *Ars Morendi* ("The Art of Dying") is the name given to a fifteenth-century pamphlet believed to have been created and distributed extensively throughout Europe by Catholic priests in order to assist people suffering from the plague in preparing for a good death. This is explored more thoroughly in chapter 5.

expected to provide spiritual guidance to lay people, particularly in times of distress. In her research on caring for terminally ill individuals, Helen Kruger outlines the "needs of the dying patient," the first of which, she says, is the need for opportunities "to discuss the process of dying, body changes, losing control, *and what happens after death.*"[7] She elaborates by asserting that "a strong sense of spirituality is the best coping resource for the dying process."[8] Christopher Vogt suggests that a Christian facing death needs to be able to express care for his/her caregivers; to engage in other-directed activities while also receiving care; to experience patience, compassion, and hope throughout the dying process.[9]

Yet many hospitalized individuals currently seem to die in emotional or spiritual distress amid what is generally referred to as *heroic* or *aggressive medical measures* that can end up inflicting physical and emotional suffering,[10] preventing people from dying in peace as they otherwise could. Even people who receive hospice care, either in their home or in a nursing care facility, at times opt to be hospitalized after a fall, sudden shortness of breath, or some other unexpected incident in order to receive more intense medical interventions—likely a decision prompted by end-of-life fears and anxieties. Our current culture tends to be one of trust and hope in the medical establishment, commingled with an extreme fear of death, which results in considerable existential/spiritual distress.

It has been said that "Christians must be given a method of directing their own passing to a happy eternity," with which I concur.[11] I posit here that there must be a more optimal model for twenty-first-century chaplain intervention than that which tends to be the

---

7. Kruger, "Caring for People Who Are Terminally Ill," 158. Italics have been added by me for emphasis.

8. Kruger, "Caring for People Who Are Terminally Ill," 159.

9. Vogt, *Patience, Compassion, Hope, and the Christian Art of Dying Well*, 111–20.

10. Physical suffering could include (but is not limited to) chest compressions, intubation, transfer to ICU. Emotional suffering would involve depression and anxiety.

11. O'Connor, *The Art of Dying Well*, 6–7. See also: Campbell, "The Ars Moriendi: An Examination," 9.

## An Elaboration of the Dilemma

present norm: the reflective listener adept at quietly delivering a ministry of presence, a model potentially ideal for the latter half of the twentieth century, but that perhaps is in need of reconsideration in these changing times.

The Protestant Christian belief that grace is available for all points to the chaplain's potential to be a spiritual conduit, helping those perched on the precipice of death to confront their own mortality, recognize their own ability (or opportunity) to "penetrate to the kingdom of truth," and permit the peace of Christ to enter their souls.[12] This ministerial responsibility stems from the growth of both religious pluralism and secularism in this country. Hospital chaplaincy emerged in the USA during a time when the majority of people (individuals and families) maintained membership with a given church. At this point in time, however, a significant shift has occurred such that this is no longer the case. For example, *more than 50%* of residents in the Philadelphia region claim *no* affiliation. Currently, individuals may acknowledge being raised in a certain tradition or belief system, but they no longer claim that faith or belief in their day-to-day existence.[13] With this type of shift, the religious language fluency people one had seems to be dying, creating a need for chaplains to exercise scriptural language more frequently and more confidently than in years past, in order to help the dying individual give expression to his/her situation and access spiritual reconciliation and peace before death.[14]

---

12. Weil, *Waiting for God*, 64. Weil wrote that any human being "can penetrate to the kingdom of truth . . . if only he[/she] longs for truth and perpetually concentrates all his[/her] attention upon its attainment. . . . When one hungers for bread, one does not receive stones"—a beautifully articulated sentiment that seems particularly poignant in relation to individuals readying themselves for death.

13. See http://www.city-data.com/county/religion/Philadelphia-County-PA.html. The survey analyzes data for "Philadelphia County, PA" from the 2010 census, comparing it to 2000 census information. As of 2010, 51.2% of Philadelphians claimed not to be "religious adherents" to any specific tradition or faith identity—a 280% increase from 13.6% in the year 2000.

14. I draw upon Brent A. Strawn's cogent claim that "the Old Testament is dying" in identifying the loss of religious/scriptural language. Strawn notes that "Just as language . . . allows us to make sense of the world and ourselves,

## Peace Be with You, Rest in Peace

As a case in point, when I entered the field of chaplaincy in 2008, families confronting the imminent death of a loved one would often recite the Lord's Prayer as effortlessly as breathing. As the years passed, I noticed that one member of a family may initiate the prayer, or may ask me to begin it, but fewer and fewer of the others in the room were able to join in. Eventually—in the past few years—families might ask me to say the Lord's Prayer, but themselves are unable to remember much of it. At times, I find that I am the only one in the group who seems to know it, which makes it feel as though I am speaking Latin. I share the Lord's Prayer before a gathering of silent, vacuous stares. Perhaps occasional words here and there are familiar to those gathered, but the fluency has been lost.

I feel convinced that the incorporation of Scripture into critical conversations with terminally ill individuals assists them in confronting their unresolved anxieties, specifically by delivering to them the language they need, ultimately helping them attain a sense of peace *before* dying, in order to truly "rest in peace." Finding and speaking the right theological words at the precise time they are needed most assists individuals with the resolution of their lingering concerns, fears, and anxieties by replacing doubts with affirmations that have transcended centuries. As ordained ministers, chaplains should not shy away from such pivotal moments in the name of honoring the "ministry of presence" model—or even as a result of what may have become a habitual tendency toward this type of quiet, reflective-listener ministry over years of one's chaplaincy. Habit or routine may inadvertently come across as complacency and detachment, like one just coasting in neutral, too disengaged to shift gears. It is our duty and privilege to facilitate the entering of the peace of Christ into others' souls—to be the spiritual conduit that permits others to penetrate to the kingdom of truth, and permits the kingdom of truth to penetrate others.

---

the Old Testament provides a kind of grammar" to help us interpret our surroundings and predicaments (Strawn, *The Old Testament Is Dying*, 8). I would expand this thought to argue that Scripture in its entirety provides this grammar; if one loses that language, s/he turns to those believed to be linguistic experts to help her/him access the language again.

An Elaboration of the Dilemma

## RE-ENVISIONING CHAPLAINCY FOR SPECIFIC PATIENTS/ENCOUNTERS

An ever-increasingly secular society with ever-advancing medical technology needs—and seems to long for—ministers adept at providing the spiritual language and the words of peace that the secular mainstream now lacks. The very language itself has been lost—or if not entirely lost, at least temporarily forgotten due to lack of use. An unfortunate amnesia has developed over recent decades. And as such, the judicious, respectful, well-planned inclusion of Scripture into pastoral care visits with terminally ill patients receiving palliative treatment could (in my opinion) provide the guidance, words of comfort, and reassurances of peace that individuals in the process of transitioning into the kingdom of truth desperately crave.[15]

It has been said that individuals who have faced stressful situations in the past "with open confrontation [as opposed to denial] will do similarly in the present situation,"[16] thus availing themselves to conversations about end-of-life existential concerns. Therefore, if the seasoned chaplain seizes certain opportunities to address a patient's expressed concerns, then suggests reading select Scripture passages prior to honoring that patient's request for a word of prayer, this may help the patient address her/his anxieties and fears more conclusively. I reiterate that this should first be *suggested* to the patient (for example, by saying, "As you were sharing your story with me, a certain passage came to mind . . .") because I do *not* subscribe to the thought that it is acceptable to impose one's religious beliefs onto another—particularly another who is in a vulnerable situation. I believe in living by example, in trying to respect others' beliefs and feelings, and in periodically offering certain possibilities to assess the other's receptivity in as ethical a manner as possible.

Something that Elisabeth Kübler-Ross said back in 1969—that "dying nowadays is more gruesome in many ways, namely, more lonely, mechanical, and dehumanized"[17]—only seems to have grown increasingly poignant over time. The dying process in the United

---

15. Weil, *Waiting for God*, 64.
16. Kübler-Ross, *On Death and Dying*, 45.
17. Kübler-Ross, *On Death and Dying*, 21.

## Peace Be with You, Rest in Peace

States has become more and more complicated (and consequently lonelier and more dehumanizing) in recent decades. Interdisciplinary team members working closely with palliative care team specialists tend to be quite concerned about patients' increased feelings of isolation, hopelessness, and "deep depression from which [they] may not emerge unless someone is able to give [them] a sense of hope."[18] Some medical professionals specifically identify this as *spiritual distress*, and have come to rely on well-trained chaplain ministers to assist the patients with such spiritual/emotional crises. And yet, it has been noted that chaplains are at risk of "spiritual 'drift' [with] dangers of 'dumbing down the spirit'"[19]—a phenomenon I feel I have witnessed firsthand, both in myself and in the other chaplains in my midst. It is strongly suggested that chaplains become mindful of this phenomenon, opting to embrace "a more considered engagement . . . with theological roots and resources."[20] I couldn't agree more. The spiritual drift creeps in slowly, imperceptibly, dulling the senses and cognitive prowess of the chaplain, who was once so remarkably attentive. It takes a conscious effort—a sort of shaking the dreams awake—to alert oneself to the phenomenon as it descends over the chaplain's spirit.

Thus, this study aims at being that type of conscious deliberation, incorporating reflections and quotes from chaplain encounters with people diagnosed with terminal and/or metastatic cancer, all of whom were cared for by palliative care team specialists (physicians and nurse practitioners). The reflections specifically revolve around the role of select Scripture passages in chaplain-patient (one-on-one) encounters. And although palliative care tends to focus on pain management (and not "comfort measures," per se), this study spans a two-year timeframe with patients whose diagnoses are *terminal*. As such, most of the individuals represented here had died by the completion of this project.

Finally, while reading this work, one must keep in mind the backdrop of the contemporary "dying with dignity"/"medical aid

---

18. Kübler-Ross, *On Death and Dying*, 48.
19. Swift, *Hospital Chaplaincy in the Twenty-First Century*, 74.
20. Swift, *Hospital Chaplaincy in the Twenty-First Century*, 74.

## An Elaboration of the Dilemma

in dying" movement that had been gaining momentum (both philosophically and litigiously) prior to the onset of the COVID-19 pandemic. This was in part due to the national publicity of Brittany Maynard's last several months of life prior to her death in 2014.[21] The number of states in the U.S. that have death with dignity statutes nearly doubled during the course of my research.[22] Evidence suggests that end-of-life concerns—and the desire for a peaceful transition from this realm—are among the most critical aspects of life one could ever consider. Why not turn to Scripture for guidance?

---

21. In recent years, a shift in mindset has begun to transpire wherein people are reclaiming their own abilities and rights in the end-of-life decision-making process. Brittany Maynard was a twenty-nine-year-old, diagnosed in 2014 with a glioblastoma, a fast-growing, deadly form of brain cancer, who made very deliberate decisions to determine how to spend her last few months of life. See http://www.cnn.com/2014/10/07/opinion/maynard-assisted-suicide-cancer-dignity/index.html. See also the Compassion and Choices website: https://www.compassionandchoices.org/research/speakers/speaker-dan-diaz/, through which her husband, Dan Diaz (a lawyer), continues to promote "medical aid in dying." The Compassion and Choices website notes that "Dan advocates for expanding the availability of end-of-life options for terminally ill, mentally capable individuals."

22. In 2016, there were five states with death with dignity laws. There are now eight states, plus Washington, D.C. Additionally, although Montana does not have a statute in place, its Supreme Court has ruled that nothing prohibits physicians "from honoring a terminally ill, mentally competent patient's request by prescribing medication to hasten the patient's death." See https://www.deathwithdignity.org/learn/death-with-dignity-acts/.

3

# Encounters

## Patient Relations, Artifact Analysis

To say, "It wasn't easy determining which patient situations might be best or most appropriate for the vision of ministry I had hoped to cultivate," would be a tremendous understatement. Frequently, I would ponder the suitability of each new patient I encountered, often thinking I had found someone who might be a "good match" for my ideas about building rapport and pinpointing special Scripture passages that resonated with the given circumstance, only to discover that the patient had been discharged from the hospital much sooner than originally anticipated (either by her/his own choice to seek other treatment options elsewhere, or because there was a change in the medical plan). But fortunately, I started early enough in the process that time was on my side. After all, like a good marathon runner, I was able to pace myself—and had approximately two and a half years in which to create a viable pool of individuals for my research/reflections!

With that being said, I eventually was able to build solid pastoral relationships with fourteen individuals. And I firmly believe that building such relationships is key. For each case, I required of myself a minimum of three ministerial encounters through which I could build rapport and trust. I have included reflections on five of those relationships (or "case studies") in this section; the remaining nine can be found in the Appendix. The names of all individuals have been changed[1] in order to protect their privacy and respect the Health Insurance Portability and Accountability Act of 1996 (HIPAA) regulations.[2] The patient pool I discuss incorporates a variety of ethnicities and age ranges, as well as a striving for gender balance; however, the majority of the individuals ended up being females of European descent, in part because there continues to exist among non-Euro individuals and families a hermeneutic of suspicion regarding palliative and hospice care.[3] All patients included for reflection in this study consider themselves to be Christian (either Protestant or Catholic) and voluntarily identified themselves as such immediately after I introduced myself; yet they represent the broad spectrum of varying degrees of involvement in a home church.

When I embarked upon this study, I surmised that there would likely be one ideal, pivotal Scripture passage that would function well for all patients. As a former special education teacher who believes whole-heartedly in individuality and the individualization of educational instruments or pedagogical approaches, I'm honestly not sure how I could have been so naïve! I suppose that my heart or my emotional intelligence must have assumed that either Psalm 23 or the Lord's Prayer (the "Our Father") was the absolute perfect balm for any spiritual, physical, or medical ailment. Perhaps these *are* common "go-to" passages. And perhaps their relative familiarity

---

1. In creating pseudonyms for each patient, I selected biblical names whose meanings seemed to resonate with each individual's unique personality. This is made fairly evident with my use of the name "Miriam" for someone who had been a dancer and singer as a young adult, for example.

2. See https://www.hhs.gov/hipaa/index.html for more information about HIPAA rules and regulations.

3. Publications such as Rebecca Skloot's *The Immortal Life of Henrietta Lacks* address this nation's collective history of manipulating people of color and people of minority status in ways that have benefited the medical establishment. Mistrust stems from "historical racism, forced sterilization of black women, and the infamous, government-led Tuskegee syphilis experiment that denied effective treatment to black men" (Bailey, "Taking on Planning for the End of Life").

and thematic content *do* bring comfort to those in distress. But by the close of the first patient encounter reflected upon here ("Leah"), I realized that what was appropriate for Leah would likely *not* be appropriate for others. I quickly opted to go back to the proverbial drawing board, modifying and adapting my approach. Using the Individualized Education Plan/Program (IEP)[4] as my model, I created an informal, quasi-equivalent, theologically rooted plan for monitoring the progress of the research process. The notion of developing of an Individualized Scripture Plan[5] for each patient revealed itself to me as the most judicious approach. As an added perk, it would simultaneously honor the years I had spent working with exceptional students and people with special needs (intellectual and/or learning disabilities)!

The Individualized Scripture Plan, as I envisioned it, would be based on each person's unique spiritual, emotional, and even social needs. Ministerially speaking, I felt convicted that the best—if not only—way to honor someone's dying needs was to be critically attentive to her/his personal expressions, interests, beliefs, and desires. This approach was (and is) admittedly intuitive in nature and does not necessarily follow a specific $a + b = c$ type of formula. In the same vein as creating pseudonyms for each individual based on his/her emotional affect and interests, the scriptural passages I selected tended to be based on deductions drawn from the first two encounters I had had with each. Although the lectionary texts became a reference point for me (which will be explained in greater detail later), a minister nonetheless has the opportunity to choose from several lectionary passages in preparing a sermon and worship

---

4. According to the *Medical Dictionary for the Health Professions and Nursing*, an IEP can be defined thus: In the U.S., an education program tailored to a particular student with a disability, the provision of which is mandated by law. Mandated by the Individuals with Disabilities Education Act, an IEP has two parts: the plan itself and the written document supporting it. See *Medical Dictionary for the Health Professions and Nursing*, https://medical-dictionary.thefreedictionary.com/Individualized+Education+Plan (accessed on January 6, 2018).

5. To the best of my knowledge, this is not already an existing term. I created this term based on what I perceived as its close correlation to the Individualized Education Plan/Program of the U.S. educational system.

service. The passage ultimately chosen for each individual patient (even when consulting the lectionary) was based on my own intuitive sense about that person's spiritual and emotional needs (or, in other words, upon asking myself, "I wonder which text would resonate most closely, deeply, and profoundly with this person?").

## CASE STUDIES/PATIENT ENCOUNTERS

The five individuals chosen for this section are referred to as Leah, Miriam, Gemariah, Cyrus, and Abigail. Each required considerable medical attention necessitating several week-long inpatient hospitalizations (usually approximately one week per month). The palliative care team maintained a computerized calendar of their patients' re-admittance schedules in order to help them track each cycle of medical care. As a member of their interdisciplinary team, I had the privilege of being able to coordinate my own plans based on knowledge of these patient schedules, medical goals of care, and patient progress through the treatment plan. Thus, like my former teacher self, I was able to consider objectives for each visit with a given patient, and could determine a methodology for building rapport with each over time, while bearing witness to their physical, mental, emotional, and spiritual changes throughout the process.

## Leah[6]

Leah was a Filipino woman, seventy-one years of age, a self-described Evangelical. She was the first patient within the parameters of this study to whom I said, "Would it be helpful if I read some Scripture with you?" Even from my first encounter with her, she made it clear that prayer helped ease her pain and assuage her anxiety. As I have found to be the case with most individuals over the span of my chaplain ministry, she did not have any particular biblical passage in mind, but rather relied on me to choose a text for her.

---

6. One translation for the Hebrew name, "Leah," is weary. This patient seemed very weary from her trials.

## Peace Be with You, Rest in Peace

Per the suggestion of a fellow chaplain who had also once visited with her, I selected the passage from Matthew 26:36–42.[7] Like Jesus in this passage, she never gave up hope that it might be possible that God would "let this cup pass" from her and permit her recovery, even as physicians continued to provide difficult medical news of her cancer's progression. She repeatedly expressed feeling hopeful that God might respond to her plea, remove her pain, and at least impede the growth of her cancer (if not remove it all together). As I read aloud the words from verse 39 ("let this cup pass from me; yet not what I want but what you want"), she stopped wincing from her pain for a brief moment. I chose to repeat that verse a second time, and then a third. I then continued reading up through verse 42, at which point I took a risk in asking her directly if hearing these words was helpful.[8] She nodded affirmatively, whispered, "Yes, yes." But after several moments of silence and calmness, she then cried out in pain again.

Unbeknownst to me, this would be the last time I would see her. I learned the next day that she was discharged to hospice that evening, only hours after I had been with her. I never saw her again. I can only hope that correlating her situation to that of Jesus at Gethsemane (via this Matthean text) helped assuage her end-of-life anxieties and provided some affirmation that God was with her in all things.

Admittedly, although this passage did seem appropriate for Leah's situation, there was something extremely disconcerting for

---

7. Matt 26:36–42 (NRSV) depicts Jesus at Gethsemane. According to Matthew's version of this incident, each time Jesus prays, his prayer involved an element of hope: "he threw himself on the ground and prayed, 'My Father, *if it is possible*, let this cup pass from me; yet not what I want, but what you want'" (v. 39); and "he went away for the second time and prayed, 'My Father, *if this cannot pass* unless I drink it, your will be done'" (v. 42).

8. Chaplains are educated to avoid asking questions to the greatest extent possible, the rationale being that every other hospital professional asks a litany of questions. It is the chaplain's role to be "safe space" from interrogation. Chaplains tend to attempt to frame all expressions in a statement or observation form. (For example, saying, "It seems like you feel sad," or "That could feel overwhelming," rather than "How does that make you feel? Are you sad?") Another aspect of this theory is that questions can at times feel like loaded judgments; by avoiding questions we hopefully embody the absence of judgment in the encounter.

me about reading it to a dying person. Consequently, she is the only person for whom I selected a "Garden of Gethsemane" passage. After that, I set about diligently brainstorming ideas for what it might entail to create an Individualized Scripture Plan for each patient I encounter. It would be less about consulting with colleagues for suggestions or ideas, and more about trusting my intuition in purposefully, carefully reflecting upon each person's unique story to discern Scripture passages that echo aspects of their humanity, their individuality, and their life narrative.

## Miriam[9]

From the first few minutes of my initial encounter with Miriam, I felt a particularly deep, personal obligation to help her navigate her diagnosis. A seventy-year-old Protestant woman of European descent, she suspected that the cause of her cancer could be traced to the Lockheed-Martin engineering plant near where she lived in Moorestown, NJ—a corporation that employed my father for over twenty years. Miriam was a very artsy individual who had been a dancer in her younger years. She spoke of "rubbing elbows" with celebrity dancers such as Gene Kelly, Debbie Reynolds, and Donald O'Connor. She also openly indicated that she would need to figure out how to draw upon her own waning inner strength in order to confront her terminal situation, as her husband was emotionally not able to be strong for her.

The reflective listening I employed with Miriam tended to mirror the creative spirit and inner strength that I witnessed within her, with which she apparently feared she was losing touch. I thought she would benefit greatly from some simple reminders about her own core strength. I determined that Exodus 15:1–21[10] had the potential

---

9. One of the meanings for the Hebrew name, "Miriam," is "beloved." To me, this individual not only seemed in love with all of creation, but also seemed to *be* loved *by* creation—and by the Creator.

10. Exod 15:1–21 (NRSV) is a fairly lengthy passage that perhaps need not be included in its entirety here. Verses 1–19 are referred to as "The Song of Moses," proclaiming that the Lord is the source of strength and might, the greatest of warriors, who overturned Pharaoh's chariots and army. Verses 20–21

## Peace Be with You, Rest in Peace

to both resonate with her *and* inspire her. As I read, "The LORD is my strength and my might, and has become my salvation . . ."[11] and "Who is like you, O LORD, among the gods? Who is like you, majestic in holiness, awesome in splendor, doing wonders?"[12] she nodded silently. But when I reached the part about Aaron's sister, the prophet Miriam, leading a dance with tambourines,[13] her face absolutely lit up. She indicated that she had never heard this passage before. The words of celebratory dancing seemed to help her heart feel light, and to strengthen her spirit.

During the encounter in which I shared the Exodus text with her, she had been out of bed (for the first time since I had met her), seated in the recliner chair in her room; the lights had been off, the room darkened, and she had a somber, almost hopeless expression on her face. However, the next time I saw her a few days later (which also happened to be the *last* time I saw her), she was ambulating down the hall with a nurse assist on one side, with an expression of peace and relative joy on her face. A smile even periodically flashed across her lips. She is one individual I firmly believe I helped by employing a more active form of ministry: by genuinely hearing her story, finding a passage from Scripture that might resonate with it, and affirming her in the fullness of her humanity. It is my deep conviction that the Individualized Scripture Plan that was created for her helped pull her out of a dark emotional place by reminding her of who she is, affirming her gifts, and allowing her to see that she has much yet to give—and to live.

---

are then "Then Song of Miriam" which notes that "The prophet Miriam, Aaron's sister, took a tambourine in her hand; and all the women went out after her with tambourines and with dancing. And Miriam sang to them: 'Sing to the LORD, for he has triumphed gloriously; the horse and rider he has thrown into the sea.'"

11. Exod 15:2, NRSV.
12. Exod 15:11, NRSV.
13. Exod 15:20–21, NRSV. See footnote 35.

## Gemariah[14]

I first met Gemariah less than an hour after he had reconciled the medical concern that he would be "DNR/DNI" and seek no further treatment options.[15] He felt that the time had come for him to confront his own mortality and begin saying his goodbyes. Even as I sat with him and his wife in his hospital room, an oncologist came in to discuss this decision with him, to ensure that Gemariah fully understood, beyond any shadow of doubt, any and all ramifications of his choice. On a second visit, after listening to his emotional/spiritual concerns and ruminations, I prayed with him and his wife for strength, clarity of mind, the opportunity to have meaningful conversations/closure with loved ones, and peace. Only moments later, his three children (ages fourteen, nineteen, and twenty one) arrived.

My third visit with Gemariah involved his wife, their three children, and a longtime friend who were all present in the room. He asked if I would pray with all of them, at which point I requested his permission to read from Scripture before we prayed together. Realizing that Gemariah and his family identified as Catholic, I took a moment to discuss the Protestant lectionary system with them, then noted that Psalm 147 was among the optional readings for that upcoming Sunday (January, 2018). "With your permission," I said, "I would like to read parts of this psalm for you before we pray." He and his wife both smiled and said they thought that would be very nice.

I read Psalm 147, vv. 12–16 and 20.[16] Then I paused for a moment of silence and reflection before leading them in a prayer about

---

14. Germariah may be translated from Hebrew as, "God has accomplished." I feel that this individual accomplished the admirable feat of confronting and reconciling all significant issues and life-matters within the few days-to-weeks prior to his death. As such, God accomplished admirable feats through him.

15. In medical language, these abbreviations stand for "Do Not Resuscitate/Do Not Intubate."

16. Ps 147:12–16 and 20 (NRSV) reads, "Praise the Lord, O Jerusalem! Praise your God, O Zion! For he strengthens the bars of your gates; he blesses your children within you. He grants peace within your borders; he fills you with the finest of wheat. He sends out his command to the earth; his word runs swiftly. He gives snow like wool; he scatters frost like ashes.... He has not dealt thus with any other nation; they do not know his ordinances. Praise the Lord."

## Peace Be with You, Rest in Peace

the beauty and blessing of Gemariah's own family, his children, and the keen intellects both he and his wife possessed. I followed this with a word of petitioning for God's peace and strength to sustain them all in the days to come. Being that his children were in the room listening to all that I said, I recognized the extraordinary nature of the reference to God blessing the children (of Zion) in verse 13 seemed for the situation. Gemariah did not cry. Instead, after the prayer, he relied on his intelligence and his where-with-all to begin sharing some of his knowledge of early ancient Near Eastern religions with everyone gathered. He informed them that, during the past two years as he drove to and from chemo treatments, he managed to listen to an audio version of the entire Bible a minimum of two times, probably more. (He lost count.) Everyone listened quietly and attentively, imprinting in my mind the image of disciples gathered around the dying man's bed, gleaning wisdom from him during his last days of life, his last words, his last breaths. It felt at the time like both a profoundly intense *and* intensely profound moment.

Gemariah was discharged from the hospital to home the next morning. His wife called me four days later to let me know he had died peacefully the day before. She also wanted to thank me, to express that my involvement in his care was deeply appreciated. Indeed, she affirmed that the visits were as pivotal for him (and them) as it felt for me.[17]

---

17. He was discharged from the hospital on 01/05/2018 to home hospice care. His wife had called to let me know he died peacefully at home three days later (01/08/2018). She then visited the hospital on 01/26/2018 "to thank a few of his caregivers," naming me as one who made a tremendous impact on him and the family. According to his wife, my last visit (on the afternoon of 01/04/2018) in which I read Scripture and then prayed with them was the impetus for this typically quiet, reserved man to begin giving voice to things in life he found to be most important. It facilitated conversations of forgiveness and closure, bringing him a sense of peace. Later that evening (January 4th), when it was just him and his wife, he shared with her a list he had made concerning funeral logistics, what he wanted to wear, who it was important for him to see again before he dies, etc. His wife attributed this "opening up" to my reading of Scripture and my subsequent prayer. She identified this one moment as being exactly what he needed in order to address these critical things before dying. "In that one final act," she said, "you brought faith to him

## Cyrus[18]

Sixty-year-old Cyrus is arguably one of the most fascinating characters with whom I have ever had the pleasure of crossing paths. He was an enigmatic African American man who identified himself as Protestant Christian but expressed multifaith perspectives that included a respect for Jewish and Muslim faith traditions. He frequently spoke of the Qur'an, Torah, and Bible collectively in one breath. During each of my visits he seemed to take much glee in sharing with me his belief that God is a woman, that God wants peace and harmony, but that man creates war. "But," he would say, "that's all right. Out of chaos, order is born." And from there he would launch into discourse about various religious writings (such as the book of Genesis). Although in my mind he was "only sixty," he expressed that he felt ok about dying. He spoke at length about death in terms of atoms—how we are all made up of atoms, and when we die, we will continue to exist as atoms. In fact, he identified our ongoing presence in atoms as "the true stuff" of the resurrection, articulating an intriguing integration of theology with science and math in metaphysical inter-relatedness.

My numerous encounters with Cyrus consistently felt reminiscent of conversations I had participated in throughout an elective seminary course on the Wisdom Literature. Therefore, it's no surprise that I felt inspired to draw from Ecclesiastes for him. I introduced a passage from Ecclesiastes 3 to him by saying, "Are you familiar with this writing? The band The Byrds, had a popular recording in the 1960s that used this text:[19] To everything, there is a time and a purpose under heaven—a time to be born, a time to die . . . ." He instantly lit up: "Oh, yeah! I know that song!" Then I

---

when his faith was wavering. You helped him find his way." In my opinion, this is concrete evidence of how significant this research is.

18. Cyrus can be interpreted as, "Far-sighted, young." This individual had a life-altering experience as a teenager. In addition to that, he struck me as very youthful and jovial in his affect and attitude.

19. The Song, "Turn, Turn, Turn," is attributed to Pete Seeger, who composed it in the late 1950s. The band The Byrds popularized the tune in the mid-1960s with the release of their recorded version in 1965. See http://www.songfacts.com/detail.php?id=246 (accessed on January 12, 2018).

skipped down to Ecclesiastes 3:10–15[20] and said, "This is what it says just after that . . . ." He listened as I read slowly and methodically through the verses. "That's *it!*" he exclaimed. "*That's* what I'm talking 'bout!"

I do not necessarily believe that my incorporation of Scripture into our visits impacted him on a deep, significant, life-altering level the way it seemed to for some other patients. Cyrus appeared to have reconciled his own end-of-life anxieties and potential fears on his own terms, at his own pace. He seemed genuinely relaxed and at peace with his own transition-to-death process. Reading Scripture with Cyrus was less about helping him confront or resolve anxiety prior to death, and more a means of affirming him in the fullness of his humanity. But the validation he received by my pinpointing a passage that spoke directly to him seemed to help create a strong rapport between us which would not have existed had I remained in a ministry of quiet presence. In other words, with him, I became more than just a good listener. I became his pastor.

## Abigail[21]

On the evening of "Super Bowl Sunday" (February 4, 2018), during an overnight shift, a nurse paged me to ask if I could spend time with fifty-three-year-old Abigail. I had recently become familiar with this patient's name and medical circumstances, but had not yet introduced myself to her. As I entered her room, Abigail

---

20. Ecclesiastes 3:10–15 (NRSV) states, "I have seen the business that God has given to everyone to be busy with. He has made everything suitable for its time; moreover he has put a sense of past and future into their minds, yet they cannot find out what God has done from the beginning to the end. I know that there is nothing better for them than to be happy and enjoy themselves as long as they live; moreover, it is God's gift that all should eat and drink and take pleasure in all their toil. I know that whatever God does endures forever; nothing can be added to it, nor anything taken from it; God has done this, so that all should stand in awe before him. That which is, already has been; that which is to be, already is; and God seeks out what has gone by."

21. The Hebrew name, "Abigail," can be translated as "My father rejoices." From what I perceived and what I knew of this individual, I believe God rejoices very much in her being and in the way she has lived her life.

*immediately* expressed gratitude for a pastoral care visit. A devout member of her United Methodist Church in Leesburg, Virginia, she had come to this Philadelphia hospital specifically for the expertise of its neuro-oncology physicians and medical staff. She had received the diagnosis of a glioblastoma—potentially the worst (most aggressive, most fatal) form of cancer one could have—in October, 2017. She felt painfully aware that "the clock was ticking" for her, since the average lifespan from time of diagnosis is thirteen months. After sharing details of her life story with me (including mission trips to Mexico and the Dominican Republic, as well as living in Afghanistan for thirty months as part of her job within the auditing department of the federal government), she asked me to pray for her. She squeezed my hand tightly, almost as if for dear life. She requested not a prayer of healing, but rather one of strength—the strength it would take to face each day with gratitude, with clarity, and with dignity. She confided that what she sought most was discernment on how to use her own diagnosis—her own suffering—to help ease the suffering of others who might find themselves in a similar situation.

On the second visit, she shared that she was born and raised in California. She ended up in northern VA (Manassas) for work, and decided to settle there. About fifteen minutes into this visit, a hair stylist contracted by the hospital came to her room per her request to have her head shaved. I stayed nearby in order to gauge her comfort or anxiety level with this process. I have known countless women for whom this act caused immense unanticipated grief, emotional pain, and many tears. Abigail, however, came across as brave, strong. She shed no tears. She simply said she was "ready."

My third and fourth visits with her were fairly brief. But during the fifth visit, she revealed emotional vulnerability again. She spoke of the results of her colonoscopy, tying it into her concerns about having to stay in the hospital longer than originally expected. She mentioned not understanding why it was part of God's plan for her to contend with this diagnosis. Yet she continued to express a deep conviction she was being called to help others going through similar circumstances or experiencing comparable forms of personal suffering.

## Peace Be with You, Rest in Peace

I had come to her room prepared with a one-page Word document I had created that consolidated several passages from Paul's second letter to the Corinthian community.[22] As I pulled the folded piece of paper from my pocket, I introduced it to her by saying, "I hope you don't mind . . . ," I paused, then continued, "but I wove together a few passages from Second Corinthians for you. I remembered you saying a few days ago that you were struggling with the concept of suffering. I wanted to find a text that would resonate with those feelings." She nodded, and in fact began to cry—I think because she was caught off-guard by my attentiveness to her, by the way I had followed up on this previous conversation, and by the fact that I had heard her—truly heard her—in a way that validated her feelings. She seemed surprised that I had brought this to her, *specifically for her*. I surmise that my deliberation helped her feel authentically valued at a time when she felt isolated and lonely. Additionally, because she was aware that the GBM (or the chemo treatments, or both) was/were impacting her short-term memory, she expressed gratitude that I had produced the passages for her in written form, which she could keep to read and re-read as needed or desired.

I only had one more visit with her before she was discharged from the hospital. I had brought with me a print-out of Psalm 103, but left it out in the hall closet in order to assess whether it would be something she might want in that particular moment.[23] For the most part, this visit seemed fairly "light" in nature. But toward the end, Abigail gave voice to one of her primary fundamental beliefs. She stated that even though suffering is painful, she felt there must always be some reason for it. Likewise, she believed there must always be some reason to give thanks in the midst of suffering, or in

---

22. The passages from 2 Corinthians include 1:3–7; 3:17–18; 4:5–8, 16–18; and 6:16–18 (NRSV). In pondering an Individualized Scripture Plan for her, these sections seemed most appropriate. These resonated closely with her life story.

23. From my perspective, chaplains ought to regard spiritual assessments not as a one-time inventory, but rather more of a living, breathing document that is open to change. I came prepared, but wanted to informally assess the patient's current situation to discern whether the time was right. This is part and parcel of being an ethical, respectable, and perceptive chaplain—and, in my mind, human being.

spite of the suffering. In all things, give thanks. With that, I asked her if she would mind if I shared with her a "Psalm of Thanksgiving." She said she would deeply appreciate that. And with the reading aloud of Psalm 103, my final visit with Abigail came to a close.

## ARTIFACT ANALYSIS

Any type of decent research should help interested onlookers become aware of the parameters, limitations, and other considerations with which the study had to contend. In this case, I want to be explicit in stating that every aspect of this study is specific to one particular level-one trauma center teaching hospital in the Philadelphia region of Pennsylvania. This hospital also serves as an ACPE-accredited Clinical Pastoral Education site with Spring, Fall, and two concurrent Summer intern programs as well as a residency program. And, fortunately for me and my chaplain colleagues, this context supports the full-time functioning of a handful of staff chaplains.

A number of parameters were considered and created from the outset. After much deliberation, I determined that these three factors would be required in order for me to include a patient in this reflection/research: (1) the palliative care team is actively involved in the patients' plans of care; (2) each patient had received a terminal diagnosis; and (3) a minimum of three chaplain–patient visits must transpire as part of the ongoing assessment in determining the appropriateness (or lack thereof) of integrating Scripture into a visit with that patient. I felt (and continue to feel) that it is extremely important to respect these boundaries. Verbal and nonverbal behaviors were recorded in a journal[24] in order to assess the validity of this project's assertions. Autoethnography was the primary method of measuring and assessing myself and this approach to chaplain ministry, since analysis in this type of research hinges on observations rather than on specific quantifiable statistical evidence.[25]

---

24. For clarification, a *written* journal was kept—*not* a video or audio-recording type of journal.

25. Autoethnography is to be understood as "an approach to research and writing that seeks to describe and systematically analyze personal experience in order to understand cultural experience," as well as spiritual and religious

First, the "artifact" itself is the Scripture being incorporated into the third (fourth, fifth, etc.) encounter I was able to have with a given patient. Initially, I had thought that one specific, constant biblical passage could be utilized with all patients, that passage thus becoming the "artifact." However, as noted earlier, it became almost immediately evident after encounters with the very first patient of this study ("Leah") that this one-size-fits-all ideology was completely inappropriate. Thus, the development of an Individualized Scripture Plan for each patient became the "go-to" approach, based on each person's needs and expressions. All individualized artifacts came from either NRSV or NIV Bible interpretations. Use of the Vanderbilt Divinity Library Revised Common Lectionary was an additional component of the "artifact," since it became clear to me that patients with lengthy hospitalizations seemed to benefit from timely seasonal readings, such as those designated for Pentecost or the Season of Advent.

Next, implementation of the artifact was conducted in the manner of me, the chaplain, reading a given passage aloud to a particular patient, often repeating parts of the text or the whole text in order to add emphasis. It is noteworthy that texts were *not* selected via scrolling through the internet on my cell phone in the presence of a patient, nor by flipping through the pages of a hard copy of Scripture; rather, passages were determined ahead of time through careful, methodical planning—not unlike a teacher creating a lesson plan or a pastor creating a worship service. A specific passage was selected deliberately for a given patient *prior* to entering the room, and that passage was printed out on a plain white piece of paper.[26]

---

experience. See Ellis et al, "Autoethnography: An Overview."

26. During the first few months of my CPE residency in Atlanta, I once walked through the hospital with a Bible, preparing to visit with a few patients. More than one staff chaplain saw me and advised that "Carrying around a Christian Bible doesn't help us present ourselves as interfaith ministers . . . ." Therefore I find it significant to mention that I did not walk into patients' rooms carrying a Bible; I carried only a folded-over white sheet of paper— which in itself stands in contrast to the way I typically carry absolutely nothing in my hands. Even if I was headed directly to a patient's room, the concern persists that others (patients, families, staff) would see the Bible and formulate instant judgments about it.

Each visit was planned in advance, and each passage was perused several times during the planning process in order to consider both potential positive *and* negative aspects of reading the passage to the patient.[27] Throughout the planning, several translations were considered (NRSV, NIV, NKJV, ESV, New Jerusalem Bible) in order that the one chosen might have the optimal intended effect of helping the person process her or his end-of-life circumstances by instilling or facilitating a calming sense of peace.

Another tremendously significant aspect of the implementation of Scripture that cannot be reiterated enough is that *never* did I, the chaplain, walk into someone's room and immediately begin reading a biblical passage to him/her. I employed the standard ministry-of-presence model *consistently*—100% of the time—until the minimum of three chaplain-patient encounters provided sufficient evidence that offering to read Scripture to the patient would quite likely be well-received. This was generally determined through comments made by the patient regarding spirituality, prayer, or theological insights/musings. But prior to presenting the possibility of sharing a passage from Scripture, the patient's mood, affect, and even mental/physical/medical condition that day were all carefully (albeit informally) assessed: Was the patient nauseated? Did s/he have a fever? Were the lights out, shades drawn, and the blanket pulled over his/her head? Or did s/he seem to welcome the chaplain into the room, talk freely and uninhibitedly, and generally present himself/herself with an attitude of openness and receptivity to the pastoral care visit? Each and every one of these environmental factors matters immensely.

One final consideration of this study is that much of its implementation occurred shortly before or during the Advent season and into the season of Epiphany. It is plausible that the Advent season itself could have subconsciously or unconsciously impacted each individual's receptivity of Scripture. There tends to be a sense of readiness—or of openness—that accompanies the anticipation of

---

27. Throughout the planning process, I asked myself a series of significant questions: "Does this passage seem too adversarial? Does it invoke (false) hope? Could it provoke depression? Or (as was my primary goal), is it a passage that the patient will likely feel gives expression to what he/she is feeling?"

the birth of Christ. Even if people feel depressed or overwhelmed by their illness (particularly in combination with the very short days and long nights, i.e., less sunlight), they still seem to be seeking, hoping, longing—emotions that permit one to lower one's guard, lending oneself to an openness through which the Holy Spirit may enter. Or, in the words of the well-known Christmas hymn, "No ear may hear his coming, but in this world of sin, where meek souls will receive him still, the dear Christ enters in."[28]

Innumerable lessons could be (and were) learned from the entire process of engaging Scripture in an ethical, non-imposing manner with people who were cognizant of the fact that they were dying. Perhaps the most critical of all things learned is that in our contemporary, highly secularized socio-historical context, a hospital or hospice chaplain may be the *only* minister a dying person has at this point in his/her life. The chaplain may be the one-and-only minister available to this person, to help her or him become emotionally, mentally, and spiritually prepared for death. And, as I noted in the first section, it is quite possible that a chaplain can help individuals achieve internal peace by assisting them with confronting and accepting the reality of their own imminent death,[29] by facilitating a life review, by affirming the fullness of their humanity, and by giving them the (spiritual/emotional) tools to allow them to resolve any lingering concerns or fears.

On a personal note, I learned that I feel much more valid as a chaplain and pastoral/spiritual care-giver when I conceive of myself as a minister adept at speaking directly to a person's heart and soul by delivering the word that s/he seems to desperately need. More specifically, I feel more effective as a chaplain minister when I am actively striving to keep the language of Scripture alive in the midst of dire circumstances, where it is arguably needed the most—on the precipice of death, where words of comfort, peace, hope, and affirmation are paramount. A final invaluable lesson learned is that the ministry of presence may unlock and open the door into a castle

---

28. Brooks, "O, Little Town of Bethlehem," written while serving as an Episcopalian minister at Holy Trinity Church in Philadelphia, PA, between 1862 and 1869. See https://www.britannica.com/biography/Phillips-Brooks.

29. Kübler-Ross, *On Death and Dying*, 31.

frigid with fear and anxiety, but delivering appropriate and timely Scripture can in essence turn on the heat in the castle, making the environment warm, comfortable, safe, and even like home.

And in end-of-life circumstances, I believe that is exactly what I am expected and ordained to do: to be a shepherd ensuring the safe passage of God's sheep back to our Creator. How disconcerting it feels to me to proselytize to people dying in distress, for the spiritual distress is a form of deep suffering. A "good death"[30]—one in which a person feels prepared to die—honors the phrase many of us say to one another on any given Sunday: "May the peace of Christ be with you."

---

30. See Neumann, *The Good Death*.

# 4

# Reflections

## INCLUSION OF SCRIPTURE VS. ABSENCE OF SCRIPTURE IN PATIENT ENCOUNTERS

My goal in conducting this study was specifically to reflect on the inclusion of Scripture into prudently selected chaplain pastoral care visits with terminally ill individuals. I respect that, as a general rule, this practice tends to be discouraged in many hospital environments. One of the primary reasons for concerns and opposition to Scripture inclusion is the well-founded fear that one who walks into a patient's abode with Scripture in hand will at some point cross the line in evangelizing to a non-believer, or the problematic ministerial approach of claiming that biblical texts can cure whatever ails an individual as long as s/he believes deeply enough. Suffice it to say that prayer, "God language," and use of Scripture tend to be absent from pastoral care visits, particularly for hospital chaplains. A Rogerian person-centered approach to pastoral care visits remains the norm.[1] Inpatient environments prioritize the safety, comfort, and

---

1. Throughout my fourteen years as a chaplain, I have probably prayed with patients and/or families twenty times or less. Prayer is rarely requested; when it is offered, the majority defer to, "Just keep him/her in your prayers."

quality of life of every patient, which includes ensuring that they feel emotionally and spiritually safe.

As Allen Verhey and countless others have noted, however, this type of generic spirituality leads not only to a dumbing down of the chaplain's spirit, but arguably also to an irresponsible model of ministry. Rather than merely coasting in this sweeping, non-specific, vague approach to chaplaincy, it would greatly behoove ordained chaplain ministers to instead hone a skill set of reflective discernment to judiciously determine when to engage in a ministry of presence (i.e., most of the time) and when to assert a more proactive, lead ministerial role (i.e., for specific circumstances or particular occasions).

In ruminating over inclusion versus omission of Scripture in pastoral care visits, it seems that "no sooner than the third visit with a given patient" was/is an extremely sensible starting point. This allows for at least two previous encounters in which a chaplain can build rapport and trust with a patient while simultaneously gauging that patient's potential receptivity to Scripture, to an offer of prayer, etc. I know that, for myself (or if I were the patient), I would need to believe that the chaplain visiting with me was genuinely interested in my life story, my theological beliefs, my emotional comfort, and so forth. I would need to feel respected. And I would definitely *not* feel safe if a minister I've never encountered before entered my room with a hidden agenda of proselytization.

Scripture seemed to be of value for each of the individuals incorporated into this study, with the possible exception of one ("Keturah," whose situation is explained in the appendix; she had requested chaplaincy support to help her cope with the fear of hell instilled in her throughout her Catholic school upbringing, but over time it became clear that she primarily wanted an anonymous reflective listener and empathetic ear). However, in terms of the hypothesis that reading Scripture could be an important vehicle to help terminally ill patients confront their anxieties about death and dying, thereby developing a sense of peace and resolution before they die, it could only be said with relative certainty that nine out of fourteen individuals exhibited *clear* signs of peace and assuaged anxieties after Scripture was read with them.

## Peace Be with You, Rest in Peace

The fourteen individuals that I ultimately included in this study, as well as the impact this process of creating Individualized Scripture Plans may have had on them, are summarized below. The "yes," "no," etc., refers to the hypothesis that reading Scripture could help terminally ill patients confront their anxieties and develop a sense of peace before they die:

Leah—yes, she communicated that hearing about Jesus in Gethsemane was helpful for her.

Reuel—not really; he already indicated a sense of peace and calmness about his process; however, he expressed gratitude and pleasure upon hearing the words from Isaiah.

Rhoda—yes, Psalm 62 in fact seemed to help provide clarity in her decision to seek no further chemo treatments but rather to go home on hospice.

Keturah—no; for her, Scripture may have mentally/subconsciously transported her to her young Catholic school days, for which she was emotionally unprepared.

Miriam—yes; in fact, it may have played a pivotal role in inspiring her to get back up on her feet and seize whatever time she had left.

Lydia—yes; however, Lydia's level of anxiety continued to ebb and flow as her cancer progressed. I believe that ongoing visits with Scripture readings could be helpful to one's peace of mind in circumstances where the end-of-life process is longer and more drawn-out, such as Lydia's was. The model set forth here should have continued with a steady rhythm of planned visitations to assist her in maintaining her sense of peace over time.

Chloe—yes; although I believe it was already within her, searching for someone like a devoted pastoral care-giver to support her through her own resolution of life's challenges.

Keziah—difficult to say; for her, the simulation of Mass was what she needed. Thus, she is the one I deemed as "unclear response" in my analysis.

## Reflections

- Gemariah—yes; for although he was confronting his own DNR/DNI status, he was visibly nervous and anxious about it. Hearing the psalm with his family gathered around him seemed to provide a much-needed sense of peace and affirmation.
- Michal—yes; Psalm 80 brought peace to her heart and alleviated her fears.
- Tirzah—yes; the text from Mark 1 seemed to touch her deeply and profoundly, chasing "the devil" from her heart and thoughts.
- Cyrus—not really; he had already said he was ok with dying. Nonetheless, the passage from Ecclesiastes provided some semblance of joy in its affirmation of his thoughts, feelings, and beliefs.
- Abigail—yes; the words of Scripture alone seemed to touch her spirit and mood, but also the gift of bringing specific passages selected with her in mind seemed to mean the world to her.
- David—not really; he was quiet and resigned in terms of both verbal and nonverbal expressions (or, as medical professionals might say, he had a "flat affect"). But he is one patient who *consistently* requested pastoral care visits *every time* he was admitted to the hospital.

This information could be depicted or charted in a number of ways. Consider the following:

- Nine out of fourteen gave clear indications that it helped.
- Four out of fourteen gave indications that it did not (necessarily) help.
- One patient gave unclear indication of whether or not it was helpful.

However, it is feasible that the data could be deconstructed even more—broken down and analyzed from a few different angles. Being on a perpetual lifelong quest for truth, I opted to explore some of those angles.

For nine individuals, it seemed fairly explicit (either verbally or through their actions and nonverbal behaviors) that a positive emotional/spiritual change transpired as a result of hearing poignant words of Scripture specifically selected for each. For some, words of gratitude accompanied by a shift in affect may have been noted. For others, tears were shed, followed by a change in behavior that signified peace rather than anxiety or distress.

Then there were four about whom I stated above, "it did not (necessarily) help." The reality is that from my very first encounter with three out of four of these individuals, I could detect their already-established reconciliation to their own fates. Each possessed a perceptible degree of spiritual resolution regarding his/her own death. They may have responded positively to my visits by exuding kindness and appreciation for the companionship, and may have also expressed that the biblical readings were "nice." But it seemed to me that they had already resolved their own anxieties and confronted their mortality on their own terms. They had done "the hard work" on their own.

Only with one individual did it appear that the readings invoked latent negative memories from a Catholic upbringing that had been abandoned long ago in favor of a secular lifestyle. This patient had requested chaplain support and had stated very plainly from the very first visit that she wanted to get in touch with her Catholic roots in order to establish a sense of forgiveness and redemption. Unfortunately, somewhere along the line in her course of medical treatment, her feelings changed. Not only was hearing Scripture *not* helpful for her, but some might surmise it was hurtful in its own way. This shift speaks to the continuous need for the chaplain to pause and reassess, constantly revisiting the Individualized Scripture Plan to make modifications in the name of honoring the patient's potentially changing needs.

Regarding one final patient, I feel that our series of encounters produced somewhat ambiguous results. She had requested—and responded positively to—the in-room experience of Catholic Mass. However, the cancer had begun impacting the cognitive processes of her brain, causing periodic flashes of what medical professionals would refer to as an "altered mental status." Because she was in the throes of this altered state due to the disease progression, it seems most appropriate to me that she have her own unique category.

Her situation was not clear-cut by any means, and I have too many mixed feelings about adding her to the "positive response" group because so much with her just depended on the timing.

Thus, the following two pie charts could both apply to the data that was collected, depending on the perspective one wants to take:

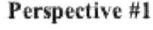

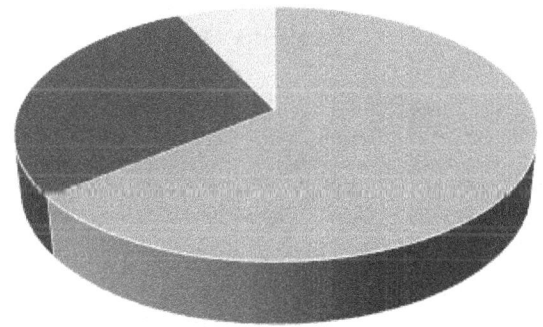

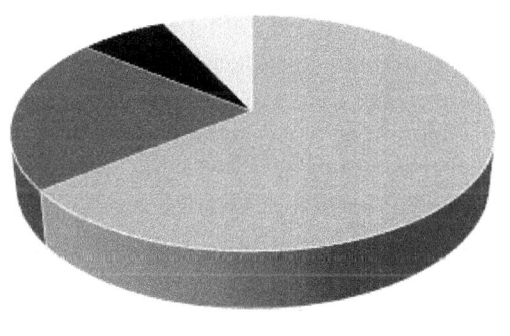

With the first perspective, it can be said that 64.3 percent of the individuals in this study demonstrated an overtly positive response to hearing Scripture, while people who seemed neutral are grouped with the negative response category due to the absence of a blatantly positive reaction. The second perspective lends itself to the possibility that, since "neutral" is actually *neither* positive *nor* negative, one could conceivably combine the 21.4 percent (neutral) with the 64.3 percent (positive) in order to assert that 85.7 percent of patients responded favorably to hearing Scripture. That information could then be depicted as such:

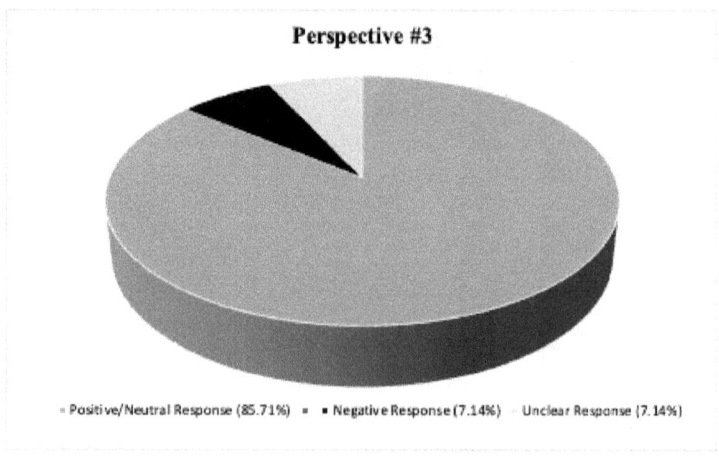

No matter how the data is conveyed or perceived, the majority of patients benefited from hearing Scripture. The question at hand, though, is how large that majority might be, since it could either be construed as a 64.28 percent majority, or an 85.71 percent majority. Naturally, when one suggests that more than 85 percent of people surveyed responded favorably to the incorporation of Scripture into certain visits, the argument sounds definitively more cogent. But either way, devising a judicious and sensitive plan to incorporate Scripture into carefully selected pastoral care visits has been demonstrated here to have considerable potential to engage patients in a much more meaningful, positive manner than visits where an Individualized Scripture Plan is nonexistent.

Given the relationships I was able to form with these patients, I would be inclined to argue in favor of the perspective that a majority of 85.7 percent of people appreciated this approach. The 21.4 percent that might not necessarily have *needed* to hear Scripture to help them resolve any spiritual anxieties or distress *benefitted nonetheless* from hearing Scripture. They were individuals who conveyed a solid Christian faith/belief system. And for each, no outside clergy person came to visit them in the hospital or called them to offer support over the phone. Thus, I became their *only* minister at this critical juncture in their lives. I was neither proselytizing nor evangelizing, but I *was* providing language that has transcended eons. The language, which evaded them when left to their own spiritual and emotional devices, seemed to reach them like a long-lost friend the very instant the words floated into their ears, assuaging any lingering end-of-life concerns.

## REFLECTIONS ON THE SCRIPTURE PASSAGES USED

The idea of using the Revised Common Lectionary to assist in selecting texts came fortuitously (but admittedly) somewhat by accident, as did the idea of creating an Individualized Spiritual Plan for each patient. And yet, it seemed to work. By reviewing the lectionary texts (including the "alternate" texts) after having already met with a given patient at least twice, it often felt fairly providential how closely a text would resonate with the patient's story. And in my mind, I anticipated each time that the text that resonated with the person's story would be the text with the greatest potential to provide comfort and extend the peace of Christ.

When I began this process of referring to the Revised Common Lectionary, I anticipated drawing primarily from the New Testament passages cited. However, as the process unfolded, I set aside this preconceived idea in order to utilize whichever texts fit the scenario best, regardless of whether the passages came from the Old or New Testament. Perhaps I initially thought that people would be most familiar with the New Testament writings, and this familiarity would foster an increased sense of peace. But what outweighed that notion was the realization that people want—and perhaps at some very base level even *need*—to feel heard, affirmed, and honored, especially when they're staring down their own mortality

## Peace Be with You, Rest in Peace

and fear of death. The text that resonates and affirms is the text that helps people "gird your loins" (as Scripture repeatedly says) for the journey at the end of this life.

Intriguingly, with the exception of a few well-known passages (such as the recounting of Jesus's baptism from the Gospel according to Mark 1:4–11 that I read for Tirzah),[2] each patient seemed fairly astounded by the poignancy of the Scripture texts. They gave the impression of being pleasantly surprised that Scripture could be so relatable and so pertinent to their own situations. I had not intended for these end-of-life ministerial encounters to be educational moments; I had only hoped they would help bring the peace that surpasses all understanding to each individual's heart. In the end, it felt like an incomparable honor to be able to bear witness to a sense of wonder that appeared in their eyes upon their hearing the salvific message of The Word.

As I reflect on the encounters themselves and on the various passages I utilized with each patient, I recognize that a minor degree of risk was involved. Myriad, countless factors are always involved in caring for others. What time of day is it? In which season are we? To what extent does the weather impact an individual's mood and/or receptivity to a pastoral care visit? Did the patient sleep well last night? Did the patient just have a difficult conversation with a loved one? Depending on the answers to these and other untold questions, I could have potentially been turned away by the patient, or the patient could have been feeling particularly hopeless and not in the mood to hear any spiritual writings.

One particularly valuable lesson I learned during my CPE residency, which I've attempted to hone over the years, is to always try to be sensitive to the other person's needs. I see it as a vital, integral aspect of taking that informal inventory upon walking into someone's room—which I tend to do not only as part of an initial visit, but of every visit. If my senses or perceptivity grow dull over

---

2. See Tirzah's story in the Appendix. Verses 10–11 of this excerpt from the Gospel of Mark seemed to resonate deeply with Tirzah: "And just as he was coming up out of the water, he saw the heavens torn apart and the Spirit descending like a dove on him. And a voice came from heaven, 'You are my Son, the Beloved; with you I am well pleased.'"

time, then I am likely to do a disservice to the other person. Thus, a key feature of consciously trying to create a viable individualized plan for each patient is that it re-awakened my senses, forcing me (in a way) to be attentive. The process heightened my sensitivities to the point that I believed I could responsibly gauge whether the timing was right or not. And if the timing felt inapt, the plan would be deferred. There is nothing wrong with choosing to pause and reassess.

As ministers, we must always be open to an unanticipated change in plans. Sometimes pastors may feel they have written the perfect sermon well in advance of the worship service, only to awaken the morning of service to discover that some major catastrophe transpired overnight. The sermon that was preached at my seminary's 11:00am worship service on September 11, 2001, certainly was not the sermon the professor had originally prepared; national events called for an impromptu word. In a similar vein, the unexpected events related to the COVID-19 pandemic threw a curve ball at ministers in this country. In the next section, I have elected to consider ways the coronavirus inspired creative ministries, and implications such a pandemic might have on the suggestions put forth in this project.

5

# The *Ars Moriendi* and COVID-19

THIS PROJECT ATTAINED COMPLETION by May 2018. But as the fates would have it, I held off on pursuing publication due to various personal circumstances. By March of 2020, with my writing/revising and editing efforts well underway, our nation found itself in the throes of COVID-19. Chaplain ministers (as well as all ministers) were forced to change their "game plan" in their approaches to ministry as churches, nursing care facilities, rehab units, and other public settings were either shut down to the public or instructed to enforce strict visitation restrictions and "social distancing" advisements. Regardless of whether the contexts were hospitals, long-term care facilities, people's private residences, or other environments, the circumstances demanded creative alternative methods of ministry. Naturally, these events impacted the whole premise of this project with its focus on individualized ministry care plans developed by building rapport with the infirm over the course of several visits.

The initial onset of the coronavirus "social distancing" demands shook everything up like a snow globe. Slowly, though, instead of settling on figurines and floors the way the imitation snowflakes do in the glass sphere, the chaotic storm became a bit of a norm. Most people found a way to adapt and carry on. And as the world kept spinning and life moved onward, ideas bestowed upon me back in January 2017 by my advisor and cherished life mentor, the highly esteemed Reverend Dr. Don E. Saliers, began echoing in my head. "Have you thought about the *Ars Moriendi*,[1] and how it might inform your current ministry and research?" At the time, this suggestion became a footnote in my studies. But three years later, amid the pandemic crisis, the synapses *finally* fired in my brain, allowing his sage advice to take center stage.

After all, this wasn't exactly the first time in history that ministers have been thrust into events in which the death toll suddenly skyrocketed. Nearly seven hundred years ago, ministers in Europe confronted a similar pandemic crisis: the bubonic plague.[2] The *Ars Moriendi* hinges upon this specific example. And whether humanity is experiencing times of relative peace or war or pandemic dis-ease, my primary goal with this exploration would remain the same: to ascertain people's dying requests/needs, to bring those supplications forth, and to develop a plan for each that would facilitate their experiencing the peace of Christ prior to drawing their last breath, so that they may truly rest in peace.

## A LITTLE BACKGROUND INFORMATION

The era of the bubonic plague provides an excellent backdrop for ruminations about contemporary spiritual care. Although there is a lack of substantial evidence about authorship, it is believed that this document (entitled the *Ars Moriendi* due to its inherent goal of helping individuals, families, and communities understand *the art of dying well*—that is, dying peacefully with an assurance that all human sins, errors, submissions to temptations, and/or regrets are forgiven) was produced and disseminated by (or at the instruction of) Dominican priests[3] in response to the immense devastation of

---

1. Latin for "the art of dying," and also a pamphlet created and distributed extensively by the priests to assist plague victims in dying a good, reconciled, peaceful death. See Osborne, "Ars Moriendi: A Selection of Texts."

2. The bubonic plague ravaged Europe and Asia in the mid-1300s. See https://www.history.com/topics/middle-ages/black-death, accessed on April 20, 2020.

3. O'Connor, "Making the Most and Making Sense," 55. It is important to

the plague. "With so many priests either dead or missing, the popularity of a manual that instructed how to die in a way that ensured one made it to heaven is easy to understand."[4]

In other words, the priests and other church officials of the day realized that their game plan had to change. People craved an understanding of the veritable art of dying well, seeking end-of-life affirmations and words of reassurance, believing in the necessity of ministerial intercession to fulfill these comfort measures. Yet it was not feasible for the limited number of priests to administer the "Last Rites" to all in need. Subsequently, they created and dispersed two versions of the *Ars Moriendi* document (a lengthier one for the literate, and a concise illustrative version for those who were illiterate) to facilitate a peaceful death by proxy, aimed at assuring believers of their salvation despite the priest's absence.

Although the circumstances during the twenty-first-century COVID-19 pandemic involve clear historical, scientific, and theological distinctions from the era of the bubonic plague, resounding parallels can be drawn. Consider the following:

- Countless people were dying so quickly in circumstances precluding ministers from being present to them that spiritual distress was a very real aspect of their end-of-life experience.

- People sought a minister's companionship and blessing to (re)assure them of divine salvation/peace after they have died.

- A shortage of priests contributed to the challenges of providing ministry to the overwhelming number of infirm within a condensed timeframe.

- Ministers began thinking creatively and utilizing alternate means to support, pray for, provide blessing/Sacrament for, and comfort the infirm.

---

remember that since the plague occurred more than a century prior to the start of the Protestant Reformation (1517), documents from that era, such as the *Ars Moriendi*, refer only to priests—not to pastors, ministers, deacons, etc. The Christian church in the West at the time was the Catholic Church.

4. Campbell, "The Ars Moriendi: An Examination," Abstract.

I will explore each of these similarities more thoroughly. After doing so, I will reflect on the pertinence of the *Ars Moriendi* and the contemporary coronavirus pandemic in relation to my convictions about the role of Scripture in certain individualized spiritual-care encounters.

## COUNTLESS DEATHS, CONDENSED TIMEFRAME, CONSIDERATIONS OF VISITATION RESTRICTIONS

Ministers during the fourteenth century and the twenty-first century alike grappled with trying to provide end-of-life spiritual care, unable to be with the dying person firsthand. In both circumstances, legions of people were dying very quickly, many of whom could not receive adequate medical interventions in time. Those seeking spiritual support were unable to receive that care directly—that is, in person. And indeed, it definitely seems as though "people need more spirituality, not less, in times of pestilence."[5]

In our contemporary context, from mid-March 2020 onward throughout the months following, hospitals and nursing care facilities enforced a "no visitors" policy that also included ministers. For people residing in their own homes as they died, they were often told by clergy (priests, rabbis, imams, chaplains, pastors, etc.) that home visits were not occurring due to COVID-19 concerns. During the plague, the limited number of priests simply were physically unable to travel far enough, fast enough, to reach the infirm in time. However, the end result of either era was the same: the dying individual who sought spiritual care was unable to receive that support in person. Their terminal anxiety and spiritual distress at times went unassuaged. Given the circumstances, many healthy and able-bodied people did the best they could in meeting the needs of the dying. However, to say that things were "complicated" would be a drastic understatement.

---

5. Collins, "Catholic Moral Theology."

PEACE BE WITH YOU, REST IN PEACE

## MINISTERIAL COMPANIONSHIP AND INTERCESSION

Next, people in each era (and people throughout history) sought a minister's word of forgiveness, of salvation, of blessing, and of peace as they lay dying. As the chaplain fielding the priest requests from our families of Catholic patients in local nursing homes, I quickly discovered that priests were granted autonomy by the Vatican to determine for themselves the risk involved in, and the prudence of, entering facilities and/or visiting with people who were "COVID-positive," as they came to be called.[6]

This seemed to lead to a bit of temporary confusion, though. Some priests indicated to me that they could provide an Absolution of sins over the phone as an equivalent of the Anointing of the Sick (formerly known as "Last Rites," which involves a priest physically administering holy oil). Other priests noted that it is not possible for either the Sacrament of the Sick or an Absolution to be honored via phone interaction because both must occur in person; they offered instead to say a prayer to/for the dying individual over the phone. Still others declined the use of phone communication with/for patients, opting instead to offer a "Chaplet of the Divine Mercy" service for the given patient, which would be broadcast live over the internet via that given church's website in order that families could stream the service live and pray along from their own home.[7] The official word ultimately dispensed by the National Association of Catholic Chaplains and the Catholic Health Association of the

---

6. Collins, "Catholic Moral Theology," March 25, 2020. The worldwide Catholic church endorsed each parish creating its own response plan. As I communicated with various priests in the South Jersey region, each seemed to feel comfortable asserting his own boundaries regarding visitation considerations with COVID-positive individuals. Nearly all of them opted for over-the-phone or internet blessings in order to avoid the risk of either acquiring or spreading the coronavirus. See also: NACC/CHA, "Questions and Answers Regarding the Sacramental Practice During the COVID-19 Pandemic."

7. See https://divinemercy.life/chaplet-of-divine-mercy/. This website notes that "Praying the Chaplet of the Divine Mercy is a glorious way to enter into the abundant Mercy of God." Often the service could be broadcast in the patient's nursing care facility room, too.

United States on March 31, 2020, was that "the priest should make every effort to administer the anointing of the sick, working with medical authorities to ensure proper protection against further spread of the virus. If it is not possible to administer the anointing, he can provide the patient the prayer of the Church, prayers for a dying person, the prayer of Apostolic Pardon, and the assurance of the Plenary Indulgence granted the person with COVID-19."[8]

But, as you can see, all of these involve a remote, virtual style of ministry. Our hospice team (nursing professionals, chaplains, social workers) became necessary intercessors in the provision of these final blessings. Chaplains were the go-betweens for families and priests. I often wondered what I would want if it were me lying there, dying from COVID-19 complications. But each family of every single patient under my care only expressed gratitude for facilitating the blessings—not disappointment that the priest was unable to be there in person, himself. All were tremendously and admirably understanding, humble, and grateful for whatever could be done.

## A DEARTH OF MINISTERS

The shortage of priests, both then and now, contributed to the challenges of providing ministry to those preparing to die. During the fourteenth century, this scarcity could be primarily attributed (a) to the high mortality rates from plague transmission while hearing the confessions and administering "Last Rites" (i.e., Anointing of the Sick) for the dying[9] and (b) to clergy that "did not always perform their duties at a time when they were most needed."[10]

---

8. See https://www.chausa.org/docs/default-source/default-document-library/qa-regarding-sacramental-practice-during-the-covid-3-31-20-(002)15289af4df f26ff58685ff00005b1bf3.pdf?sfvrsn=0. See also, "Responding to COVID-19: Answers to Questions," https://newsroom.churchofjesuschrist.org/article/responding-to-covid-19-answers-to-questions .

9. Campbell, "The Ars Moriendi," 6–7.

10. Campbell, "The Ars Moriendi," 8. Campbell goes on to note that "Clement VI issued a papal bull in June of 1349 that permitted laymen to make confessions to each other" and granted remission of sins for all who died from the plague.

## Peace Be with You, Rest in Peace

Many priests died, but some admittedly disappeared or could not otherwise be accounted for.

While priests have not necessarily been "missing" during the coronavirus situation like they were during the time of the bubonic plague, the number of individuals serving as Catholic priests and nuns seems to be at an all-time low.[11] In my own experiences throughout this pandemic, a handful of priests worked feverishly to meet the needs of considerably large regions in New Jersey. At times I would contact the Catholic church I thought was closest to a nursing care facility, only to be told by the church secretary that "our priest died a few months ago and we don't currently have a replacement," or "Perhaps you could call [the church in a neighboring township] for help since our priest is unavailable." The vast majority of the time, I was in touch with the same two or three priests for our various patient needs. I had them on speed-dial. One of the priests even joked that he came to eagerly anticipate my calls! We became a pretty good team in confronting the considerable amount of grief and loss.

### CHAOS AS THE IMPETUS FOR CHANGE

There is a longstanding adage that says, "Necessity is the mother of invention." So it is that creativity became a fortuitous by-product of the rampant spread of disease during the time of the plague, the coronavirus, and other crises throughout history. I know I am not alone in feeling that this type of phenomenon harkens back to Genesis 1:1–2, with everything in the beginning being a chaotic, formless void—until God began creating.[12]

---

11. Yellin, "Catholic Church's Challenge"; Johnson, "The Catholic Church Is Looking for (More Than) A Few Good Men"; Buckley, "NC Priests Reflect on the Future Amid a Shortage of Priests"; Martos, "Priest Shortage"; "Priest Shortage at a Glance," https://www.futurechurch.org/future-of-priestly-ministry/optional-celibacy/priest-shortage-at-glance 2010.

12. Genesis 1 (NRSV) starts with "In the beginning when God created the heavens and the earth, the earth was a formless void and darkness covered the face of the deep...."

## The Ars Moriendi and COVID-19

Relatively soon after the plague and the current pandemic each began their relentless spread, ministers recognized that people's spiritual needs were not being met. They/we responded creatively during both scenarios, utilizing alternate means to support, pray for, provide blessing/Sacrament for, and comfort the infirm. Relying on the same routines they/we had been accustomed to just wasn't an option anymore.

During our twenty-first-century pandemic, many clergy took note of incidents from history. Rather than succumbing to a near-inevitable death knell, like the priests during the early part of the bubonic plague, contemporary ministers almost immediately closed the doors to their physical places of worship and opened gathering places online for the safety and welfare of their flocks. Instead of visiting face-to-face with those dying from complications related to COVID-19, chaplains and other clergy offered spiritual support via window visits of people's residences, over the phone, or by observing the six-foot social distancing recommendations while wearing all necessary personal protective equipment (N-95 masks, face shields, gloves, gowns, etc.). Priests in the mid-1300s who visited in-person with people dying of the plague often contracted and died from the disease themselves, but modern ministers aspired to continue delivering pastoral care to their flocks while simultaneously avoiding and preventing any inadvertent spread of infection.

The *Ars Moriendi* was born as a creative ministerial response to meet the spiritual needs of the day. Family members shared prayers and inspirations from the leaflet to their dying loved ones to reassure them that they would attain salvation, and to help them die peacefully with their lingering end-of-life concerns reconciled.[13] Similarly, our contemporary shortage of priests led to chaplains utilizing the online Zoom video communications tool to

---

13. The *Ars Moriendi* included five temptations of the devil that one experiences near death; five corresponding inspirations from angels; advice on how to die as Christ died; general instructions for those gathered with the dying person; and a series of prayers. Campbell notes, "It is not a text of great intellectual prowess or literary beauty." It was a document of function, intended to assuage spiritual anxieties/distress, and to ensure spiritual salvation upon death. See Campbell, "The Ars Moriendi," 5–6.

facilitate virtual encounters whereby one priest could bless numerous patients within a short period of time from a remote location, and the families of each patient could bear witness to that process from their own home.[14] Chaplains made the "Chaplet of the Divine Mercy" services possible for patients and families by communicating these needs to the few priests available and then informing the family members when, where, and how to access the online worship service devoted to their loved one. In short, the chaplains initiated myriad creative ministries to conquer the chaos, that death might lose its sting.[15] And somewhat unexpectedly, the consistent response that I and other chaplains received from families and loved ones was not disappointment or angst over what could theoretically be viewed as a substitution for the "real" thing; it was immense gratitude and understanding. Across the board, people graciously accepted the accommodation to the previous ritual with which they had always been familiar.

## THE *ARS MORIENDI*, THE CORONAVIRUS, AND THE HOPE FOR INDIVIDUALIZED SCRIPTURE PLANS

So how does all of this pertain to the proposed considerations about developing Individualized Scripture Plans for/in certain spiritual care encounters? What happens when "the best-laid schemes o' Mice and Men"[16] (i.e., people) go astray? Is it still possible to cater one's ministries to the personal needs of the terminally ill individual? I asked myself each of these questions as I prepared to publish my doctoral project. And after much deliberation, I determined that it is *always* essential to (a) be attentive to an individual's needs, and (b) consult Scripture for guidance. I

---

14. See https://zoom.us/about/ for more information about Zoom. Other electronic mediums included Facetime, Skype, and video options on people's cell phones. However, most of the people I was in contact with used Zoom.

15. Isa 25:8 (NIV), "he will swallow up death forever"; 1 Cor 15:55 (NIV), "Where, O death, is your sting?."

16. Burns, "To a Mouse," July 1786.

turned to Scripture in attempting to resolve these queries. Scripture advised me that if the clergy person has one hundred sheep and loses one, it would be best to go after the lost sheep until it is found and reunited with the flock.[17] Be mindful of the one in need. Focus on the individual.

Although this pandemic has caused my ministry to feel reminiscent of an elementary school relay race—one in which it is us versus the Grim Reaper—I have been able nonetheless to adapt my ideas of individualized ministry to the circumstances and context. Undeniably, since March, 2020, there has been a pressing need to rush the mediation of end-of-life ministries even in the hospice realm, such that it feels akin to the crisis ministry of a hospital emergency department or intensive care unit. The cloak of unconsciousness maneuvers swiftly with COVID-19, often followed soon after by death. Thus, I had to determine a way to move ever more deftly myself.

For those in my flock who ascribe to a Christian faith system, the adaptations involved trying to facilitate the peace of Christ amid the more sudden onset of terminal agitation. The privilege afforded to me under "normal" circumstances of being able to build rapport over time had become frequently nonexistent. The needs became immediate, urgent. Fortunately, I had already discovered that the Revised Common Lectionary is a uniquely beneficial resource. It seemed only natural to continue leaning on the lectionary texts in developing an individualized plan for someone with very little time left on earth.

One thing I was *not* able to do throughout the first two or three months of the pandemic, however, was become familiar with the dying person face-to-face, facilitating a life review directly with her/him over the course of several visits. The enforced visitation restrictions and required social distancing rules precluded that from being possible, as did the rapidity with which infected people were dying. I relied on phone conversations with families and loved ones to help paint a picture for me about the

---

17. Luke 15:4 (NIV), "Suppose one of you has a hundred sheep and loses one of them. Doesn't [s/he] leave the ninety-nine in the open country and go after the lost sheep . . . ?"

individual's life story, gifts, priorities, values, and so forth. True, the intimacy of the sacred chaplain-patient bond of trust had been forsaken, but hopefully the individual's deepest existential needs were nonetheless being met. I relied on the individual's loved ones to share significant aspects of the person's life story. Then, upon gleaning from them whether the person would likely desire a verse from Scripture and a word of prayer, I felt relatively confident about selecting a text that could facilitate peace, reconciliation, comfort, and faith in salvation.

Another point that adroitly hit home was that time is of the essence. In the past, I had generally found it to be most prudent to wait until an individual felt comfortable with the medical staff's introductions before I introduced myself. Typically this only involved waiting a few days at most, and afforded the patient time to process her/his initial thoughts and feelings. However, in these COVID times, with intense urgency in the air, I wasted no time in introducing myself to family members of those testing positive for the coronavirus who sought our palliative care and hospice services. At times, family members informed me that I was the first one from the team to reach out to them. But 100 percent of the time, they expressed gratitude for my self-introduction and became immediately forthcoming about the infirm individual's beliefs and desires. Whereas during normal circumstances people in this country tend to avoid conversations about death and dying, in this time of crisis and chaos they seemed infinitely more willing to express vulnerability and accept the reality of impending death. Thus, that much more quickly could I devise an Individualized Scripture Plan for their loved one and meet his/her spiritual needs.

And all the while, I felt as if I myself had a copy of the *Ars Moriendi* in my pocket and the history of the plague as my searchlight. Armed with texts that have transcended thousands of years, and yet have been neglected and forgotten in recent decades, I maintain hope and faith that the peace of Christ reaches the people to whom we proactively minister. It has been said that "preparing to die is the final battle between the powers of good and evil";[18] these documents from past times can continue to assist those confronting their own mortality, that they might experience a *good* death—a peace-filled death.

---

18. Vermandere et al., "The Ars Moriendi Model for Spiritual Assessment," E295. This team of medical professionals in Belgium utilized the *Ars Moriendi* Model as a spiritual assessment tool for patients receiving palliative care.

6

# Humble Conclusions

AT THE RISK OF tedious redundancy, something I had noted in the third section seems worthy of repetition: the critical awakening gleaned from this study is that the chaplain may very well be the *only* minister a dying person has at this pivotal juncture in her or his life. To rephrase, the chaplain may be the only minister available to help a dying person become emotionally, mentally, and spiritually ready for his or her own transition from this life into the next realm. The chaplain, being an ordained minister, either currently possesses the ability or can develop the skills to help individuals achieve internal peace as they enter this transition process.[1] The chaplain must work diligently to remain attentive to each individual's spiritual needs, never succumbing to the perils of complacency, spiritual drift, and/or a dumbing down of the spirit.

Personally speaking, I learned an enormous amount through this process of intentional attentiveness. One of the most noteworthy learning curves was that by striving to become a minister adept at speaking directly to a person's heart and soul by delivering the Word that s/he seems to desperately need, I felt (and continue to feel) much more valid as a chaplain and pastoral/spiritual

---

1. Kübler-Ross, *On Death and Dying*, 31.

## Humble Conclusions

care-giver. In the CPE realm, I would say that this process helped me hone my own ever-growing and evolving sense of pastoral authority. I found that I feel more effective as a minister when I am actively endeavoring to keep the language of Scripture alive in the midst of dire circumstances where it is potentially most needed: on the precipice of death. I have witnessed first-hand how transformative the biblical words of comfort, peace, hope, and affirmation can be for an individual facing her/his final days or hours, who had identified with the Christian faith tradition but had become relatively inactive as a practicing Christian or felt otherwise disconnected from the church. I have taken more ownership of the reality that I might be the only minister a person has. I have also come to recognize that I might be the one person s/he relies upon for help with confronting the final chapter of her/his life. And just as I, an ordained Christian minister, have focused my efforts on self-identified Christian individuals being cared for by the palliative care team, I would speculate that similar practices might be plausible for Jewish chaplains ministering to Jewish patients, Muslim chaplains ministering to Muslim patients, Buddhist chaplains ministering to Buddhist patients, and so on.

While it is true that the ministry of presence generally establishes a fundamental starting point, builds rapport, earns trust, quietly conveys compassion, and ideally offers an absence of judgment or a "safe space," it is also true that delivering appropriate and timely Scripture verses could be the key to resolving an individual's spiritual/existential anxiety or distress. It could offer the spiritual, existential truth that death does *not* have the final word. It could cause death to lose its sting.[2] It could be the true divine in-breaking of the phrase we so often exchange on Sunday mornings: Peace be with you.

---

2. See Isa 25:8 (NIV) ("He will swallow up death forever"); Hos 13:14 ("I will redeem them from death"); and 1 Cor 15:54–56 ("When the perishable has been clothed with the imperishable, and the mortal with immortality . . .").

# Appendix

*Reuel ("Friend of God"):* A very kind-hearted forty-seven-year-old African American man, Reuel identified himself as Protestant Christian. He had suffered the effects of esophageal cancer for a few years by the time I met him. My encounters with him consistently felt deeply moving. I had initially attempted to meet him several times without success (he was sleeping, or out at physical therapy, or in a procedure). But when I finally *was* able to meet him, I found our visits to be quite memorable and engaging. Upon introducing myself and our pastoral care services, Reuel requested a Bible. After I delivered one to him, he began to talk openly about his spiritual beliefs and his desire to overcome this period of darkness in his life. He indicated that he is not a "Why me, God?" kind of person, but rather is one who says to himself, "Well, why not me?" He expressed a strong belief in humility, in counting his blessings, in loving his family, and in believing that he has it "better than a lot of people on this unit." He expressed appreciation for pastoral care support, and requested ongoing visits. Sadly, I had not even realized that he died in our hospital emergency department until I began to review his chart information for this study. The last time I saw him, he was on the oncology unit being transferred out to a rehab facility.

With Reuel, I believe I could have selected any number of Scripture passages and he would have been open and receptive to them all. But for him, I opted to search for passages that resonated

# APPENDIX

with his "Why *not* me?" frame of mind. The one I ultimately chose was Isaiah 40:28–31,[1] a passage that essentially echoes his own words of finding strength in God and being self-aware enough to realize that his faith renews his strength. "Yes. *That* is the Word. That is exactly what I needed. Read that last part again." So I repeated that even though some may grow weary, stumble, and fall, "those who hope in the LORD will renew their strength" (vv. 30–31). He began crying, but assured me emphatically that they were a "good kind of tears," that he felt deeply moved by these words. I wished I could have done more. I wished I could have taken away his disease.

***Rhoda ("Rose"):*** Rhoda was a seventy-year-old Catholic woman of European descent who, with her husband, had been leading what I would consider to be quite an enviable life of travel—not of the extravagant sort, but of the type involving camping and striving to be one with nature. For example, a few years ago she and her husband spent two months camping throughout Alaska, bearing first-hand witness to the wildlife native to each given region. I was only able to meet with Rhoda (sometimes with her husband, sometimes with just her) a handful of times over her two hospitalizations before she determined she would prefer home hospice care. During my introductory encounter, her primary desire was a visit from a Roman Catholic priest for a blessing/Anointing of the Sick. It was only through the follow-up encounters that I felt she permitted me to "journey" with her (as some say), which helped me feel confident in asserting myself to inquire if reading Scripture with her would be welcomed. Her view of her cancer treatment might be considered "realistic"—hoping for the "best," but mentally and emotionally preparing for the "worst." Her husband was ever-present throughout her hospitalizations, but he generally stepped out of her room when I would appear, waiting out in the hall in order to honor her

1. Isa 40:28–31 (NIV) states, "Do you not know? Have you not heard? The LORD is the everlasting God, the Creator of the ends of the earth. He will not grow tired or weary, and his understanding no one can fathom. He gives strength to the weary and increases the power of the weak. Even youths grow tired and weary, and young men stumble and fall; but those who hope in the LORD will renew their strength. They will soar on wings like eagles; they will run and not grow weary, they will walk and not be faint."

potential need for privacy. Each time I met with her, we prayed together per her request. Upon what would end up being my last visit, I asked if it would be ok for me to read some Scripture to her. I inquired if she had any favorite passages, but she indicated that she did not, and would be happy with whatever I selected. For her, I chose Psalm 62:1–2, 5–8, 11–12.[2] The musical, repetitive nature of the sections I read seemed to create a connection with her. She held her head down, quietly listening, as I read. When I finished, she raised her head, revealing the tears streaming down her cheeks. She reached for my hand, held it tightly, and thanked me quietly through those tears.

***Keturah ("Incense")***: This patient had an initial intrigue not unlike incense. From the first day of her leukemia treatment, she requested the assistance of a chaplain to help her make sense of everything. She was a sixty-three-year-old female of European descent, had a strict Catholic upbringing, but had been secular for years. Despite her lengthy absence from the Catholic Church, she expressed the fear that she will go to hell if she dies. I anticipated that she would be a good candidate for this study due to her eagerness to reconnect with her own articulate religiosity. However, over time and through the course of her treatment, she grew elusive like the smoke that incense produces. The pattern that developed over the course of our dozen or more encounters revealed that she primarily appreciated chaplain visits for fulfilling the role of an anonymous reflective listener—someone not involved in her typical day-to-day life like a friend or family member—or a non-priestly minister who could unofficially hear her confession to help her lay down her emotional/spiritual burdens. The first few visits, which transpired within a

---

2. Ps 62:1–8 (NRSV) reads, "For God alone my soul waits in silence; from him comes my salvation. He alone is my rock and my salvation, my fortress; I shall never be shaken. For God alone my soul waits in silence, for my hope is from him. He alone is my rock and my salvation, my fortress; I shall not be shaken. On God rests my deliverance and my honor; my mighty rock, my refuge is in God. Trust in him at all times; pour out your heart before him; God is a refuge for us. Once God has spoken; twice have I heard this: that power belongs to God, and steadfast love belongs to you, O Lord. For you repay to all according to their work."

## APPENDIX

week or two of her original diagnosis, were very Christocentric in nature. During those visits I felt comfortable assuring her that I could arrange a visit from a Catholic priest for Confession or Anointing if she desired (yet each time, she declined). I also felt it appropriate to ask her permission in reading some Scripture with her. She requested that we recite the Lord's Prayer[3] and the Catholic Hail Mary.[4] Of all of the patients included in this study, Keturah is the only patient for whom it might be said that the reading of Scripture coincided with a *reduction* in desire for spiritual support and/or an increased anxiety about her medical predicament. I would *not* assert a causal relationship between the inclusion of Scripture and an increase in her level of anxiety. However, I *can* say that in the visits subsequent to our Scripture-based visit, she seemed more detached, less comfortable, less open, and more anxious than in those prior to that pivotal encounter. This could have been a result of a number of variables.[5] But in any case, it surprised me, as I had thought that the inclusion of Scripture in my visits with her would have strengthened not only her trust in me, but also her ability to cope with the rigors of her intensive cancer treatment.

---

3. Matt 6:9–13 (ESV) reads, "Pray then like this: 'Our Father, [who art] in heaven, hallowed be your name. Your kingdom come, your will be done, on earth as it is in heaven. Give us this day our daily bread, and forgive us our debts, as we also have forgiven our debtors. And lead us not into temptation, but deliver us from evil.'" We concluded with, "Amen." Then I summarized vv. 14–15 for her as well, encouraging her that if she "forgive others their trespasses," then God will forgive her.

4. According to the Loyola Press Jesuit website, the contemporary translation is: "Hail Mary, full of grace, the Lord is with you. Blessed are you among women, and blessed is the fruit of your womb, Jesus. Holy Mary, Mother of God, pray for us sinners, now and at the hour of our death. Amen." See https://www.loyolapress.com/our-catholic-faith/prayer/traditional-catholic-prayers/prayers-every-catholic-should-know/hail-mary-prayer.

5. Among the conceivable variables resulting in this response are: existential concerns about her prognosis; impacts of the chemotherapy, which can cause behavioral changes; residual feelings or concerns about religion carried over from her Catholic upbringing; her underlying desire or need for the help of a licensed, professional secular psychotherapist.

APPENDIX

***Lydia (Paul's first European proselyte, "trader of purple fabrics"):***
There was much in Lydia's personal story that resonated directly with my own. A single woman (African American), age fifty, living alone in a two-story Philadelphia row home, no bathroom on the first floor, no family members who might be willing and/or able to aid her through her current life situation, she expressed feeling absolutely overwhelmed, isolated, and alone. Hers was a newly diagnosed multiple myeloma with a very poor prognosis (metastases to the brain, in need of a bone marrow transplant with a less than 50 percent success rate), for whom palliative care and pastoral care had both been almost immediately consulted. My introductory encounter with her felt as though it were received defensively: she responded to my offer of emotional and spiritual support with, "I'm ok. Thanks, but I'm ok." However, with each subsequent visit she began to cry more and share her feelings more freely. In other words, once rapport had been established, her level of trust seemed to increase over time. The progression of the multiple myeloma had rendered her unable to walk even a few steps (for example, from hospital bed to bathroom) without a nurse assist. She expressed that she had been raised Catholic, and takes comfort in seeing the priests around Villanova University where she works as a security guard, but aside from these infrequent and brief encounters she has no contact with a faith community or specific minister.

Unprompted by me, she openly admitted through tears during my second visit that she would like for me to help her locate passages in the Bible that resonate with her spiritual/emotional level of strength, doubt, anxiety, depression, and so forth. Thus, during our third visit, I came prepared to read to her Psalm 43,[6] which not only seemed to resonate with her circumstance, but also was listed as an alternate reading for that upcoming Sunday, November 5,

---

6. Ps 43:1–3, 5 (NRSV): "Prayer to God in Time of Trouble: Vindicate me, O God, and defend my cause against an ungodly people; from those who are deceitful and unjust, deliver me! For you are the God in whom I take refuge; why have you cast me off? Why must I walk about mournfully because of the oppression of the enemy? O send out your light and your truth; let them lead me; let them bring me to your holy hill and to your dwelling. . . . Why are you cast down, O my soul, and why are you disquieted within me? Hope in God; for I shall again praise him, my help and my God."

## Appendix

2017, in the Revised Common Lectionary. I opted to omit verse 4, though, for that line did not seem to fit her emotional mood or need at that specific time. But as I read verse 2 ("Why have you cast me off? Why must I walk about mournfully?") and verse 5 ("Why are you cast down, O my soul, and why are you disquieted within me? Hope in God, for I shall again praise him, my help and my God") to her, she energetically nodded her downcast head and muttered, "Yes, Lord!" several times in response.

I was able to visit her one more time after this, but that time it did not feel appropriate to share Scripture. That time, she needed a good listening ear to which she could cry. As of March, 2018, she continues to receive a mix of inpatient and outpatient treatments, and thus I continue to hope to share more Scripture with her at opportune times. But as for now, I feel my encounters with her have assisted her only minimally considering what might be possible over time in the future.

*Chloe ("Green Shoot"):* Chloe struck me as an open book, yet a complicated read, not unlike Chaucer's *Canterbury Tales*. She is the only patient I have ever met who asked the nurses to print out "The Daily Word" for her, to which they happily consented.[7] Like many in the Philadelphia region, she was raised Catholic and still appreciated some Catholic rituals and observances, but did not consider herself to be Catholic any longer. Somehow she was placed on our hospital Catholic census, and received Holy Communion from our Catholic Eucharistic minister volunteers, but confided in me that she didn't agree with the recitation that "we are not worthy" (which apparently one Eucharistic minister had said to her before she received the host). She believed too much in divine grace and God's love to permit herself to feel trapped in the quagmire of sin

---

7. "The Daily Word" is a website requiring an annual subscription: http://www.dailyword.com/. Each day that I visited with her, the print-out was already on her bed or meal tray, indicating that a nurse must have printed it for her by 8am. The website provides a daily reflection for its members, accompanied by a passage from Scripture. She would ask various individuals (myself included) to read and re-read the day's reflection aloud to her, that she might be able to memorize it and integrate it into the corpus of her being by the end of the day.

## APPENDIX

language, expressing instead that we are all part of God's creation and therefore are all worthy. Like Miriam, Chloe was the type of free spirit with gentle affect that seemed to garner favorable attention from the medical staff. Something about her pulled at their heartstrings. It could have been something as simple as her generous use of the phrases "please" and "thank you so much." It could have been that she had no visitors and spoke of a complicated past. It could have been that her prognosis was so bleak (the term "failure to thrive" was included in her chart). Or it could have been that after my very first encounter with her, she told the nurses each day that she would like a chaplain visit, which helped them feel they could "do" something (i.e., page me) to help this poor soul who otherwise was withering away before their eyes.

In contrast to the other patients reflected upon in this study, Chloe is the only one for whom I abandoned the process of methodically choosing a biblical passage. Because *she* had introduced *me* to this "Daily Word," it became a routine for her to ask me within minutes of my entering her room if I could read her "Daily Word" reflection to her.[8] I would begin with the Scripture passage (even though it was found *at the bottom* of the page), and then proceed to the reflection, then back again to the Scripture passage a second, third, and even fourth time. This, too, began at her prompting: "Could you read the Scripture passage again? I want to try to remember it." So in subsequent visits, I re-read the text without prompting, and found that it helped *my own* rumination of the passage while also helping her retention of it. The text was often something fairly concise, such as Proverbs 12:11.[9] After our own ritual of orally reading the reflection and biblical text, I gently provoked her to try to interpret a meaning for her own current situation. For example, with this text she contemplated working on her own past challenges, forgiving

---

8. Apparently the nurses would print it out for her and leave it on her tray table, but wouldn't actually read it to her. Her "failure to thrive" status impacted her vision as well as her energy level, so although the "Daily Word" lay in front of her, she didn't necessarily know what it said as no one was reading it to her prior to my visits.

9. Prov 12:11 (NIV) reads, "Those who work their land will have abundant food, but those who chase fantasies have no sense."

65

# APPENDIX

those she felt had abandoned her, forgiving herself for her role in whatever circumstance or misunderstanding led to their abandonment of her. She surmised that if she did the "work" of forgiveness and letting go of grudges, the "abundant food" might involve a reunification with those people about whom she expressed care. As the fates would have it, she ended up reconciling with friends, cousins, and even her estranged son. The outcome in her case truly was a beautiful story of reconciliation, brought about in large part because she allowed herself to become willing to receive help (in a variety of forms) and open to change. I dare say that had the group of us[10] not responded to her in a proactive manner, it is quite likely she would have just died alone, without these significant interpersonal conflict resolutions—which the ordained minister in me identifies as dying in a form of spiritual distress.

***Keziah ("Cassia, Cinnamon"):*** Church and her faith seem to have been the only salve for seventy-seven-year-old Keziah in her last several weeks of life. The progression of her cancer caused her to become increasingly disoriented, to the point that she once got up out of her hospital chair in her room without a much-needed nursing assist because "I have to get to Mass." The first time I met her, our encounter was no more than ten or fifteen minutes in length. A nurse referred her to me because she was worried about her mental and emotional welfare. Keziah immediately shared with me that she moved up here from Florida within the past two years in order to be close to her son and teenaged granddaughter, the latter of whom she had learned had been molested by an undisclosed family member. She was consistently short with words throughout all of my visitations with her. For example, that first encounter was so brief because she essentially terminated the visit herself by saying, "That's all I needed to say. I just wanted to get it off my chest. It took a lot for me to share that. I feel better now. Thank you." And when I replied, "Would you like to talk about it?" she would say, "No. That's all. Thank you." It seemed clear to me that the visit was done. During

---

10. That is, the multi-disciplinary team, including nurses, dietary services, myself and a few other pastoral caregivers, and members of the palliative care team.

## Appendix

the next visit I attempted to get her to explore her feelings about her cancer. She merely said, "Yeah. Well, that's how it goes. That's what I was dealt." She was not so much interested in sharing her feelings as she was in trying to simulate or recreate the routine of going to church with her sister.

It was anticipated by the oncology physicians that Keziah would need to spend no more than a week or two as an inpatient. But Keziah was admitted on October 23, 2017 and died in the hospital during that same admission on December 2, 2017. She was never able to physically make it back to church. I became her primary minister, along with our Eucharistic ministers celebrating Holy Communion with her or the priest administering Anointing of the Sick once. Since the time she was willing to spend with me was always fairly short, I chose brief Scripture passages pertinent to the imminent Advent season. Two that seemed to have the most effect were sections from Psalm 70 and Luke 4:18.[11] She didn't say much in response; she only nodded and said, "Thank you. That was nice. Thank you." As her cancer progressed within her last two weeks of life, she became increasingly disoriented; Advent music became the only non-medical balm that could calm her disquieted state. Spoken words seemed to agitate her, unless they mentioned her beloved horses, her son, her sister, or her grand-daughter. I felt grateful that she permitted me, over time, to sit longer with her and read Scripture to her. I observed that it helped relieve her anxiety—particularly Psalm 70, which I read to her on a few different occasions. It seemed to speak directly to her particular circumstance, reassuring her that God is with her. It allowed her to imagine, for brief moments, that she was in Mass, which she described as a place where she experienced a sense of comfort and of peace within herself.

---

11. Ps 70:1, 4–5 (NRSV) (from Proper 27, 11/12/2017) reads, "Be pleased, O God, to deliver me. O Lord, make haste to help me! . . . Let all who seek you rejoice and be glad in you. Let those who love your salvation say evermore, 'God is great!' But I am poor and needy; hasten to me, O Go! You are my help and my deliverer; O Lord, do not delay!" And Luke 4:18 (NRSV) (from the third Sunday of Advent, 12/11/2017): "The Spirit of the Lord is upon me, because he has anointed me to bring good news to the poor. He has sent me to proclaim release to the captives, and recovery of sight to the blind, to let the oppressed go free . . . ."

APPENDIX

*Michal ("Brook"):* Due to her extended hospitalization (more than three weeks) during the Advent season, I decided to focus on lectionary texts for the first Sunday of Advent. She had expressed feeling in a very dark place, where she felt like dying. Michal was only fifty-six years old, and had always been an enormously active individual—one who always taught herself new things and always sought growth. Only several years ago, she learned how to ride a motorcycle and bought herself a Harley-Davidson! But at this current juncture in her life, a tumor pressed on her brain, causing some paralysis on her right side, particularly her arm. She wept over the way it impacted her day-to-day functioning and robbed her of her freedom, while in the same breath she thanked God that she still had all of her cognitive faculties intact. At one point, she wondered aloud, "Where is God? Why isn't God helping me (or responding to my prayers)?" After saying that, she retracted it and again mentioned how grateful she was for the things she *did* have.

I opted to read portions from Psalm 80[12] to her on our third or fourth visit, pointing out to her some similarities between her own feelings of emptiness and separation from God with the psalmist's expressions of grief and despair. Then I prayed with her, per her request. She expressed that it helped her feel better, and she seemed much calmer. After that encounter, she also seemed to eagerly anticipate my visits. I didn't read Scripture to her every time; only on a few occasions. But I found that with her in particular, reading these passages opened some emotional door, permitted her to trust me, and causing her to look forward to our time together. In other words, it seemed to bring her a clear sense of comfort.

---

12. Ps 80:3–5, 7, 14–19 (NRSV) reads, "Restore us, O God; let your face shine, that we may be saved. O LORD God of hosts, how long will you be angry with your people's prayers? You have fed them with the bread of tears, and given them tears to drink in full measure. . . . Restore us, O God of hosts; let your face shine, that we may be saved. . . . Turn again, O God of hosts; look down from heaven and see; have regard for this vine, the stock that your right hand planted. They have burned it with fire, they have cut it down; may they perish at the rebuke of your countenance. But let your hand be upon the one at your right hand, the one whom you made strong for yourself. Then we will never turn back from you; give us life, and we will call on your name. Restore us, O LORD God of hosts; let your face shine, that we may be saved."

## APPENDIX

After the encounter in which I read Scripture to her, Michal underwent a craniotomy to have her brain tumor removed. Thankfully (and somewhat miraculously), not only was the operation successful in terms of removing the tumor; she also regained almost full mobility of her right arm, hand, and foot. I saw her again on an unexpected admission in early January, and her face actually seemed to light up at seeing me. She thanked me profusely for my ministerial presence during her previous admission, for having prayed with her, and for reading Scripture to her. She treated me as though I was her best friend, and expressed what I perceived to be genuine gratitude for my presence in her life. I don't believe my experiences with her would have felt as meaningful for her had I strictly remained in a "ministry of presence" mode.[13]

*Tirzah ("Favorable")*: I first met fifty-two-year-old Tirzah with her daughter the day after she had been admitted with a new diagnosis of acute leukemia. She'd had a history of cervical cancer from fifteen years ago, was a smoker, and had a note in her chart about alcohol-related cirrhosis, although her liver functioning seemed to be fair at the moment.

The first encounter was no more than a few minutes (perhaps due to her daughter's presence): "Hi. Nice to meet you. I'm ok right now. Thanks." Knowing she would be hospitalized for at least a month, I planned to meet with her a minimum of once per week. With each subsequent visit, she opened up more, and my length of stay with her grew longer each time. She began to increasingly express being very spiritual, "Christian" (which, given our context of Philadelphia, implied "Protestant Christian"), wanting to "put it all in God's hands," and "trusting in the Lord." During my second visit, her son was with her; but this visit averaged about twenty minutes and she requested prayer near the end of it.

She was alone during my third visit with her, which is when she broke out in tears and gave full expression to her thoughts and

---

13. Heart-wrenchingly, I was on duty when she was brought back into the hospital in severe pain, admitted directly to our Medical ICU, and died three days after admission, on 01/24/2018. I could not express to the family enough what an honor it was to have met her and spent time with her, and how sorry I was that she ended up "getting so sick."

# Appendix

feelings.[14] The visit lasted an hour. It actually was an unplanned encounter, as I had intended to spend the afternoon following up with other patients on whom I had been consulted by the medical staff. But when I saw Tirzah walking down the hall with her IV pole and a rather sullen affect, I spontaneously seized the opportunity to escort her—an encounter I later recognized as divine intervention. She shared that she was running a fever again, felt nauseated, and her spirits were low. But at the urging of her medical team, she felt she should try "doing laps," as they call it. She completed one lap around the unit but then needed to rest, so I helped her back to her room.

For the next ten minutes she attempted to uphold a brave face, saying merely, "I'll be ok. Just keep me in your prayers." At that point I continued to employ the ministry of presence and relatively silent (nonverbal) compassion, which ultimately gave way to her tears and a confession that she didn't know if she could make it. After crying for a few minutes, she engaged in a form of self-talk to encourage herself to focus on her blessings. She revealed that on New Year's Day, her nurse shared with Tirzah her own recent struggle with cancer; Tirzah noted that the nurse seemed positive through it all, so she came to see this nurse as a role model. I admitted to her that if it was me, I might struggle with depression, and that I could understand how some people might not be able to remain positive. Tirzah insightfully replied that moments like that are, in her opinion, "when we let the devil in." Although I don't necessarily subscribe to that theology, I replied, "I suppose so. I suppose you are right," which led to her expression of needing—*needing*—to stay focused on God and on positivity.

I last saw Tirzah on January 10, 2018. Throughout this encounter, she repeatedly stated, "I gave it all up to the Lord, and I feel

---

14. In my twelve years as a hospital chaplain, I have found a consistent pattern among patients coping with a difficult diagnosis: when a patient is alone, s/he tends to confide infinitely more openly and honestly with me than when family or loved ones are present. I have been told by patients over the years that sometimes they feel they need to be strong in front of their loved ones, and other times they feel that when they attempt to be honest and candid with family, family respond by saying, "Don't talk like that! You have to be strong!" essentially shutting down the conversation and leaving the patient feeling s/he has no one with whom to speak openly and truthfully.

## Appendix

much better. The devil tried to sneak in, but I gave it all up to the Lord." I elected to read the lectionary text for the previous Sunday to her: Mark 1:4–11.[15] She conveyed that she deeply appreciated hearing verse 11: "And a voice came from heaven, 'You are my Son, the Beloved; with you I am well pleased.'" After reading it, I looked at her and said, "Tirzah, God is saying to you, 'You are my child, my daughter, my beloved; with you I am well pleased.'" I repeated it again. "You are my beloved! With you, I am well pleased!" She wept, and then reached out to hug me. I prepared myself to leave her room as we chit-chatted a bit more. Then she hugged me yet again. "Thank you so much," she said. "Thank you." Again, I felt convicted that the words of Scripture helped her more than mere ministry of presence could have—although it felt obvious to me that a combination of the two (both silence *and* Scripture) over several visits was required in order to build her trust and confidence in me.

*David ("Adored, Beloved")*: I met David in May 2017, after being paged to the ICU to help him emotionally prepare himself for his wife's memorial service. (Physicians coordinated special arrangements for him to leave the ICU, participate in the memorial service, and then be immediately re-admitted back to the same ICU room.) He was originally brought to the hospital's emergency department from the scene of a motor vehicle accident. He and his daughter, who had been driving at the time, were "t-boned" at an intersection by another car. He and his daughter were on their way to the funeral home to make arrangements for his wife, who had just died

---

15. Mark 1:4–11 (NRSV) reads, "John the baptizer appeared in the wilderness, proclaiming a baptism of repentance for the forgiveness of sins. And people from the whole Judean countryside and all the people of Jerusalem were going out to him, and were baptized by him in the river Jordan, confessing their sins. Now John was clothed with camel's hair, with a leather belt around his waist, and he ate locusts and wild honey. He proclaimed, 'The one who is more powerful than I is coming after me; I am not worthy to stoop down and untie the thong of his sandals. I have baptized you with water; but he will baptize you with the Holy Spirit.' In those days, Jesus came from Nazareth of Galilee and was baptized by John in the Jordan. And just as he was coming up out of the water, he saw the heavens torn apart and the Spirit descending like a dove on him. And a voice came from heaven, 'You are my Son, the Beloved; with you I am well pleased.'"

# APPENDIX

from lupus-related ailments. He suffered a cardiac arrest as a result of the accident, from which he recuperated amazingly well. However, the battery of tests that were conducted upon admission to the emergency department revealed that he also had stage IV metastatic cancer. Thus, the palliative care professionals were quickly consulted to be part of his care team.

From my first encounter with him, I found him to be a quiet, soft-spoken man devout in his Catholic faith, who grieved the loss of his wife deeply and profoundly. Between May 2017 and February 2018, I had the privilege of spending time with him on numerous occasions/hospitalizations. And yet, throughout this time and amidst his requests for prayer, Holy Communion, and Anointing of the Sick from a Catholic priest, I never presented to him the idea of reading Scripture with him until his February 2018 hospitalization.

When I saw him in February, his words seemed more sparse, his energy level low, and his resignation to his own mortality quite evident. A psalm of lament felt apropos, so I selected Psalm 86:1–12.[16] A man of few words, he didn't say much in response. He merely seemed to listen attentively, ruminate, and then thank me for its reading. I knew that he had just moved back to the Philadelphia area from Detroit within the past year, in order to bury his wife here and to move in with one of his daughters, so I was aware that he did not have his own church community nearby. I had become his primary minister. And I can only hope and pray that I fulfilled this role adequately and with integrity.

---

16. Ps 86:1–12 (NIV) reads, "Hear me, LORD, and answer me, for I am poor and needy. Guard my life, for I am faithful to you. Save your servant, who trusts in you. You are my God; have mercy on me, LORD, for I call to you all day long. Bring joy to your servant, LORD, for I put my trust in you. You, LORD, are forgiving and good, abounding in love to all who call to you. Hear my prayer, LORD; listen to my cry for mercy. When I am in distress, I call to you, because you answer me. Among the gods there is none like you, LORD; no deeds can compare with yours. All the nations you have made will come and worship before you, LORD; they will bring glory to your name. For you are great and do marvelous deeds; you alone are God. Teach me your way, LORD, that I may rely on your faithfulness; give me an undivided heart, that I may fear your name. I will praise you, LORD my God, with all my heart; I will glorify your name forever."

# Bibliography

Anderson, Herbert. "The Bible and Pastoral Care." In *The Bible in Pastoral Practice: Readings in the Place and Function of Scripture in the Church*, edited by Paul Ballard and Stephen R. Holmes, 195–211. London: Darton, Longman & Todd, 2005.

Bailey, Melissa. "Taking on Planning for the End of Life: A Preacher and Physician Uses Her Insight to Get Her Flock to Consider Hard Choices that Need to Be Made." *The Philadelphia Inquirer*, January 14, 2018. (accessed January 14, 2018).

Bartley, J. Brian. "The Pastoral Applicability of Person-Centered Therapy." Term paper for Trinity College at the University of Toronto, Canada, 2006.

Brueggemann, Walter. *Texts Under Negotiation: The Bible and Postmodern Imagination*. Minneapolis: Augsburg Fortress, 1993.

Buckley, Bob. "NC Priests Reflect on the Future amid a Shortage of Priests." *The Buckley Report*, September 7, 2018, 11:01am. https://myfox8.com/buckley-report/nc-priests-reflect-on-the-future-amid-a-shortage-of-priests/.

Burling, Stacey. "Bringing Science to Care at the End of Life." *The Philadelphia Inquirer*, May 22, 2016, G-1, G-5. http://articles.philly.com/2016-05-22/news/73269164_1_end-of-life-care-polst-end-of-life-planning (accessed on May 24, 2016).

Burns, Robert. "To a Mouse on Turning Her up in Her Nest with a Plough, November, 1785." In *Poems, Chiefly in the Scottish Dialect*. Kilmarnock, UK: John Wilson, July 1786. See https://www.poetryfoundation.org/poems/43816/to-a-mouse-56d222ab36e33 (accessed on June 28, 2020).

Campbell, Jeffrey. "The Ars Moriendi: An Examination, Translation, and Collation of the Manuscripts of the Shorter Latin Version," pp. 294-301. Unpublished PhD thesis, University of Ottawa, 1995.

# Bibliography

Collins, Charles. "Catholic Moral Theology Has Important Role as Pandemic Causes Ethical Dilemmas." *The Crux: Taking the Catholic Pulse*, March 25, 2020. https://cruxnow.com/interviews/2020/03/catholic-moral-theology-has-important-role-as-pandemic-causes-ethical-dilemmas/.

Diaz, Dan (husband of Brittany Maynard). Phone interview/conversation by author, Philadelphia, July 25, 2017, 10am–11am EST.

Dostoevski, Fyodor. *The Grand Inquisitor on the Nature of Man*. Translated by Constance Garnett. Indianapolis: Bobbs-Merrill Educational, 1948.

Ellis, Carolyn, Tony E. Adams, and Arthur P. Bochner. "Autoethnography: An Overview." *FORUM: Qualitative Social Research Sozialforschung* 12.1 (2011) Art. 10, from http://www.qualitative-research.net/index.php/fqs/article/view/1589/3095 (accessed on February 24, 2018).

Emanuel, Ezekiel J., and Justin E. Bekelman. "Is It Better to Die in America or in England?" *The New York Times Opinion Pages*, January 20, 2016, A-25. http://www.nytimes.com/2016/01/20/opinion/is-it-better-to-die-in-america-or-in-england.html?_r=0 (accessed on May 25, 2016).

Fowler, James. *Stages of Faith: The Psychology of Human Development and the Quest for Meaning*. New York: Harper Collins, 1981.

Halpern, Scott D. "Toward Evidence-Based End-of-Life Care." *New England Journal of Medicine* 373 (2015) 2001–3.

Hutt, Karen. "The 'What Is' and 'What If' of Chaplaincy." *The Canvas Online*, November 19, 2018. https://blog.unitedseminary.edu/the-canvas/the-what-is-and-what-if-of-chaplaincy (accessed on June 24, 2020).

Johnson, Alex. "The Catholic Church Is Looking for (More Than) a Few Good Men." *NBCNews*, September 23, 2018, 4:32pm. https://www.nbcnews.com/news/us-news/catholic-church-looking-more-few-good-men-n903041 (accessed on May 1, 2020).

Kalanithi, Paul, and Lucy Kalanithi. *When Breath Becomes Air*. New York: Random House, 2016.

Kilner, John F., Arlene B. Miller, and Edmund D. Pelligrino. *Dignity and Dying: A Christian Appraisal*. Horizons in Bioethics Series. Grand Rapids: Eerdmans, 1996.

Koenig, Harold G. *The Healing Connection: The Story of a Physician's Search for the Link between Faith and Health*. Philadelphia: Templeton Foundation, 2000.

Kruger, Helen. "Caring for People Who Are Terminally Ill." In *Spiritual Caregiving in the Hospital: Windows to Chaplain Ministry*, edited by Leah Dawn Bueckert and Daniel S. Schipani. Kitchener, ON: Pandora, 2006.

Kübler-Ross, Elisabeth. *On Death and Dying: What the Dying Have to Teach Doctors, Nurses, Clergy, and Their Own Families*. New York: Simon & Schuster, 1969.

Lartey, Emmanuel Y. *In Living Color: An Intercultural Approach to Pastoral Care and Counseling*. London: Jessica Kingsley, 2003.

# Bibliography

Lazenby, Mark, Ruth McCorkle, and Daniel P. Sulmasy. *Safe Passage: A Global Spiritual Sourcebook for Care at the End of Life*. New York: Oxford University Press, 2014.

Leas, Robert. "A Brief History." The Association for Clinical Pastoral Education website: https://www.acpe.edu/pdf/History/ACPE%20Brief%20History.pdf (accessed on December 10, 2017).

Levering, Matthew, ed. *On Christian Dying: Classic and Contemporary Texts*. New York: Rowman & Littlefield, 2004.

Martos, Joseph. "Priest Shortage: Can Laypeople Lead a Parish? Look to Louisville for a Thriving Example." *National Catholic Reporter*, July 11, 2019. https://www.ncronline.org/social-tags/priest-shortage.

McEntyre, Marilyn Chandler. *A Faithful Farewell: Living Your Last Chapter with Love*. Grand Rapids: Eerdmans, 2015.

McCormick, Thomas R. "Spirituality and Medicine: Ethical Topics in Medicine." University of Washington School of Medicine, 1998. http://courses.washington.edu/bh518/Articles/spirituality%20and%20medicine%20ethical%20topic%20In%20medicine.htm (accessed on December 10, 2017).

Miller, Melvin E., and Alan N. West, eds. *Spirituality, Ethics, and Relationship in Adulthood: Clinical and Theoretical Explorations*. Madison, WI: Psychosocial, 2000.

National Association of Catholic Chaplains & Catholic Health Association of the United States. "Questions and Answers Regarding Sacramental Practice during the COVID-19 Pandemic." https://diocesehelena.org/wp-content/uploads/2020/04/Questions-and-Answers-regarding-sacramental-practice-during-the-COVID.pdf (accessed July 25, 2020).

Nepo, Mark. *Seven Thousand Ways to Listen: Staying Close to What Is Sacred*. New York: Atria, 2012.

Neumann, Ann. *The Good Death: An Exploration of Dying in America*. Boston: Beacon, 2016.

Nolan, Steve. *Spiritual Care at the End of Life: The Chaplain as a "Hopeful Presence."* London: Jessica Kingsley, 2012.

Nouwen, Henri J. M. *Our Greatest Gift: A Meditation on Dying and Caring*. San Francisco: Harper Collins, 1994.

Nussbaum, Jerry. "Interdisciplinary Teamwork: The Role of the Chaplain." In *Spiritual Caregiving in the Hospital: Windows to Chaplain Ministry*, edited by Leah Dawn Bueckert and Daniel S. Schipani. Kitchener, ON: Pandora, 2006.

O'Connor, Sister Mary Catherine. *The Art of Dying Well*. New York: Columbia University Press, 1942.

O'Connor, Thomas St. James. "Making the Most and Making Sense: Ethnographic Research on Spirituality in Palliative Care." *Journal of Pastoral Care and Counseling* 51.1 (1997) ?–?.

Osborne, Andrew. "Ars Moriendi: A Selection of Texts Concerning the Phenomenon of Death." Tacoma, WA: University of Puget Sound, 2013. http://soundideas.pugetsound.edu/book_collecting_essays/4 (accessed April 5, 2020).

# Bibliography

Puchalski, Christina M. *A Time for Listening and Caring: Spirituality and the Care of the Chronically Ill and Dying.* New York: Oxford University Press, 2006.

Purnell, Douglas. *Conversation as Ministry: Stories and Strategies for Confident Caregiving.* Cleveland, OH: Pilgrim, 2003.

Rosenberry, Q. Gerald. "Terminal Anxiety and Psalms of Lament." Unpublished DMin thesis, Princeton Theological Seminary, 1989.

Seeger, Pete. "Turn, Turn, Turn." On *Folk Songs for Young People.* Folkways. 1959, 33⅓ rpm.

Siler, Mahan. *Letters to Nancy: Re-frames That Mattered.* Macon, GA: Nurturing Faith, 2020.

Skloot, Rebecca. *The Immortal Life of Henrietta Lacks.* New York: Crown, 2010.

Sonenshine, Tara. "Dying Words: Talking about the End of Life." *The Huffington Post,* April 5, 2016. http://www.huffingtonpost.com/tara-sonenshine/dying-words-talking-about_b_9616596.html (accessed on April 6, 2016).

Strawn, Brent A. "The Designated Reader Revised: Doctor of Ministry Project Design Workshop Sermon." Sermon delivered at the 9am worship service in the Candler School of Theology Teaching Chapel, Emory University, Atlanta, August 14, 2017.

———. *The Old Testament Is Dying: A Diagnosis and Recommended Treatment.* Grand Rapids: Baker Academic, 2017.

Sweet, Victoria. *God's Hotel: A Doctor, A Hospital, and a Pilgrimage to the Heart of Medicine.* New York: Riverhead, 2012.

Swift, Christopher. *Hospital Chaplaincy in the Twenty-First Century: The Crisis of Spiritual Care on the NHS.* Farnham, UK: Ashgate, 2009.

Thiermann, Sarah Elisabeth. "If I Should Die before I Wake: An Investigation of Nontraditional Spiritual Approaches to Working with the Dying." Unpublished PhD thesis, Temple University, 1991.

Vanderbilt Divinity Library (a division of the Jean and Alexander Heard Library). Online Revised Common Lectionary: https://lectionary.library.vanderbilt.edu/ (accessed daily from September 15, 2017 through March 15, 2018).

Verhey, Allen. *The Christian Art of Dying: Learning from Jesus.* Grand Rapids: Eerdmans, 2011.

Vermandere, Mieke, Franca Warmenhoven, Evie Van Severen, Jan De Lepeleire, and Bert Aertgeerts. "The Ars Moriendi Model for Spiritual Assessment: A Mixed-Methods Evaluation." *Oncology Nursing Forum* 42.4 (2015).

Vogt, Christopher P. *Patience, Compassion, Hope, and the Christian Art of Dying Well.* New York: Rowman and Littlefield, 2004.

Walters, Kerry. *The Art of Dying and Living: Lessons from Saints of Our Time.* Maryknoll, NY: Orbis, 2011.

Weil, Simone. *Waiting for God.* New York: Harper & Row, 1951.

Wright, Alexis A., Nancy L. Keating, et. al. "Family Perspectives on Aggressive Cancer Care Near the End of Life." *Journal of the American Medical Association* 315.3 (2016) 284–92.

## Bibliography

Yellin, Deena. "Catholic Church's Challenge: A Worsening Shortage of Priests." *Poughkeepsie Journal*, June 13, 2019. https://www.poughkeepsiejournal.com/story/news/local/2019/06/13/catholic-churchs-challenge-worsening-shortage-priests/1435315001/.

www.ingramcontent.com/pod-product-compliance
Lightning Source LLC
Chambersburg PA
CBHW070325100426
42743CB00011B/2557